Contents

Identification Solutions for Behaviour by Jan Poustie   ISBN 1 901544 82 6

Word from the Author

There is an old Native American saying that says that you need to walk in my moccasins and see through my eyes before you can understand me. I very much hope that this book, and the case studies within it, enables the reader to do just that and so gain a much greater understanding of the conditions found within it. I hope that this leads to much better provision and support for those students and families whose lives are so deeply affected by the presence of these conditions.

Whilst reading through this book, you may realise that it is likely that you (the parent/adult/professional) and/or your child have some of the conditions that are mentioned within it. For some of you it might explain much of what has happened in the past and what is happening now, and for some that may seem quite devastating and be a very traumatic experience. If this is the case, it is important to remember that there has been no change in you and/or your child since you picked up this book - just a change in your perception. There is a network of help, support, advice, assessment and intervention available to you which this book will help you to find and access. The information that you gain from this book will not, in itself, fulfil your hopes, dreams and aspirations, but it may be the first step towards their realisation.

The conditions found within this book are commonly seen together; some individuals have three or four of the conditions and each condition will vary in severity and have a different impact upon the individual. **Autistic Spectrum Disorder** (ASD) which includes **Asperger's Syndrome**, has a major impact upon the individual; most will need support throughout their lives. **Attention Deficit Hyperactivity Disorder** (ADHD), with or without hyperactivity, can cause huge problems in learning and in making social relationships. **Tourette Syndrome (TS)** causes distress to those who have the condition, their carers and may distress those around them. In a society of soundbytes, of everyone wanting to achieve everything in a moment, how many are prepared to look beneath the surface of someone with this condition. To ignore the tics (utterances - obscene or otherwise and the involuntary movements) and see the real person within. TS has a considerable impact upon the life of the individual though, as some of the case studies show, it is often the presence of one of the conditions commonly seen alongside TS such as **Obsessive Compulsive Disorder**, ASD or ADHD which has the greater impact on the life of the person at different stages of life.

Individuals who have the conditions within this book can make the best of professionals and parents look, and feel, totally inadequate. Professionals that cope with the students who have the conditions found in this book are the best, families that survive these conditions are the

Parents and professionals often feel that they are at a disadvantage because the world of special needs has its own vocabulary which is forever changing. Various terms are used to describe the students who have the conditions found in this book; e.g.

- SEBD (Social, Emotional and Behavioural Difficulties),
- BESD (Behavioural, Emotional and Social Difficulties),
- EBD (Emotional and Behavioural Difficulties).

Many of us who have Dyspraxia have, like me, the EFA Metabolic Induced form of Attention Deficits. Sleep problems are a common feature when attention deficits are present and so I also have this problem. So many thoughts going on at once, my mind rarely reaches the calm that I see others reach. Catching my thoughts as they dance past my mind when I am writing my books is always a struggle; so much is elusive, so many half thoughts forgotten. Forcing my mind to stop and allow me to sleep has always been a problem, especially when I am stressed. Herbal and homeopathic remedies can help; e.g. Avena Sativa (from homeopaths) and hops and Valerian can help too (from chemists and herbalists; in Kent you can obtain the hop plants too). Herbs etc. are powerful and can have side effects; e.g. apparently Valerian can cause headaches and restlessness if used for too long a period of time. Always consult the appropriate professional before using such treatments. (Also see page 68.)

Identification Solutions for Behaviour

(including Attention Deficits, Autistic Spectrum Disorder, Asperger's Syndrome and Tourette Syndrome)

by Jan Poustie
B.Ed., (Dunelm), Cert Ed., Sharma Cert.,
R.S.A. Diploma SpLD, A.M.B.D.A.

This book was written to help both professionals and non-professionals find out the reasons why some individuals are failing to succeed and to provide information on where to turn to for help in overcoming their difficulties. It is dedicated to all those families and individuals who struggle to cope with the conditions found within this book.

Acknowledgements

We very much thank Daniel Katz MBE for his generosity in sponsoring part of the publication of this book.

Many grateful thanks go to the following medical specialists:

Dr Christopher Green: Internationally acclaimed author of books on child development and former Specialist Paediatrician, Head of Child Development Unit, Royal Alexandra Hospital for Children, Sydney, Australia and former clinical lecturer at the University of Sydney.

Dr Gavin Giovannoni: Senior Clinical Lecturer in Neuroimmunology, Institute of Neurology, University College, London.

Many thanks also go to the following agencies and organisations, and their staff:
- Afasic (Association For All Speech-Impaired Children and young adults),
- The ADHD Family Support Group UK (this group has now been disbanded),
- The Hyperactive Children's Support Group UK,
- Food Standards Agency,
- Tourette Syndrome (UK) Association,
- Jessica Kingsley Publishing (for permitting the reproduction of Tony Attwood's Australian Scale for Asperger's Syndrome).
- National Organisation on Fetal Alcohol Syndrome
- Obsessive-Compulsive Foundation
- Action for ASD

Many thanks also go to:
- **David Bowles:** Education Support consultancy which provides e-mail support for families coping with Tourette Syndrome and other neuro-behavioral issues.
- **The families and the adults who attended the Tourette Syndrome (UK) Association annual meeting in 2003** who so kindly talked to me and enabled me to have an insight into this condition and the impact it makes upon the lives of those who have it. Thanks to them, this book includes a number of case studies including ones from whole families (e.g. grandparents, parents, child and siblings).
- The extracts from *Access to education for children and young people with medical needs* (on page 50) which are Crown Copyright material are reprinted with permission from the Controller of HMSO.

The case studies in this book.
Many thanks go to the individuals and the families who are the case studies in this book. All the case studies in this book are true and the authoress hopes that by including them the reader will gain greater insight into the conditions and the impact that they make on the lives of families.

The views expressed by the authoress are her own and do not necessarily represent those who have contributed to, or assisted with, the writing of this book.

Jan Poustie

strongest. To the onlooker both groups may look inadequate; we may think that they 'let the student get away with too much'. They take a different attitude with these students, they do not try to confront them about the minor issues, instead they confront them about only the really major ones. In reality they are far from being inadequate – these are the people from whom we need to learn.

Effect on the family

The student who has a behavioural condition may upset (or even drive away) other family members, The fact that any marriages survive when just one of these conditions is present is a miracle. Parents and partners need superhuman strength of character, tenacity and vast amounts of emotional and mental strength to withstand these conditions even with good provision and support. Some are lucky, they meet excellent knowledgeable professionals who provide them with tremendous support. Others are not so lucky; these parents, children and adults meet rejection, disbelief and, in some circumstances, a complete lack of care on the part of the professionals who are meant to help them.

Effect on professionals

These conditions make great demands upon professionals. SEBDA (Social emotional behavioural difficulties association) formerly known as AWCEBD) is a multi-professional organisation which exists to promote excellence in services for children and young people who have emotional and behavioural difficulties and to support those who work with them (contact: www.awcebd.co.uk/). For far too many individuals, and their families, the outcome of the presence of the conditions in this book is misery and stress. A major cause of this situation is lack of appropriate support and provision by the professionals whom they meet. Only by providing information and training can our professionals be enabled to better understand and provide for the conditions in this book but such training may be blocked by senior staff, thus:

▸▸ one primary head teacher, in response to a class teacher's request for Asperger's Syndrome training ready for a new student entering her class, replied that she could not have the training, she was an experienced teacher so she would cope!'

▸▸ another head teacher would not allow information on ADHD training to be passed on to the teachers in the school.

All those involved with the individual need to be able to understand, and appropriately support, the individual and his/her family. However, they can only do this if they are able to identify and understand the conditions. This library has been designed to enable all parties to do just that. I hope that the information found within this book changes your life as much as it did mine.

Jan

At various points in this book the reader is referred to the other books in the library; e.g. on page 20 it says: *Can also occur with many of the other conditions found within the Profile such as Specific Language Impairment - Book 3.'* Many who read this library may have one or two of the indicators for a particular condition but this does not necessarily mean that they have this condition. (It's a bit like a sneeze does not mean that you have flu!)

Be aware of the similarities between the highly gifted individual and some of the behaviours we associate with ADHD. A gifted person may often be forgetful in daily activities simply because the mind is working on complex issues. Of course, some gifted individuals also have ADHD.

Reliable identification
It is vital that you do not just look at the checklists and/or the index but go on to look at the relevant chapters - for each condition needs to be viewed as a 'whole'. As you are referred from chapter to chapter the picture will emerge. You will usually 'know' when the full picture has emerged as it will 'feel right and complete'. Once you have read all the relevant chapters, you must then decide which of the difficulties is causing the most problems and arrange a referral for that area first, but remember that it can take months before you (or the child/adult) is seen. Please do not wait until a diagnosis has been made before contacting your relevant local help and support groups – they exist just for you, whether you are a parent, teenager, adult or professional. (They will not think that you have wasted their time if assessment shows that you or the child/adult does not have the condition.)

Identification Solutions for Behaviour by Jan Poustie   ISBN 1 901544 82 6

Specific Learning Difficulties Profile

The following conditions are found within the SpLD Profile:

THE CORE SpLD PROFILE CONDITIONS

Dyslexia (also called Developmental Dyslexia): In the past, this has been used as an umbrella term for several of the conditions found within the SpLD Profile. Nowadays, it is more appropriate to use this term only in respect of a condition where the main difficulties are with the acquisition and use of spelling and/or reading skills.

Dyscalculia

Developmental Dyscalculia: Difficulties in understanding, processing and using numerical/mathematical information. It is often accompanied by one or more of the other conditions found within the Specific Learning Difficulty Profile.

Acquired Dyscalculia: As above, but caused by conditions that are not present from birth, such as CFS/ME.
See Mathematics Solutions – An Introduction to Dyscalculia: Parts A and B by Jan Poustie (published by Next Generation).

SPEECH, LANGUAGE AND LISTENING CONDITIONS

Specific Language Impairment (also known as dysphasia)
A continuum of difficulties experienced by children and young people who have not reached expected competence in communication skills in their first language, and whose teaching and learning is consequently affected. The condition causes difficulties with expressive language (that which you speak or write) and receptive language (that which you hear or read). Often this group is defined by exclusion:

> *They are not autistic, the impairment is not the result of a physical, intellectual or hearing impairment.* (Norma Corkish, ex-AFASIC)

Auditory Processing Disorder (also known as APD and Central Auditory Processing Disorder C/APD): A dysfunction of the processing of auditory input causing problems with understanding/processing what is heard.

BEHAVIOURAL CONDITIONS

Autistic Spectrum Disorder (used to be called Autistic Continuum): Difficulties in social interaction, social communication and imagination-based activities/behaviour.

Attention Deficits (also known as Attention Deficit Disorder (ADD), Attention Deficit Hyperactivity Disorder (ADHD) and Behaviour Inhibition Disorder). Causes difficulties in concentrating/focusing attention and memorising information. It affects behaviour and has several forms.

Conditions seen alongside the Profile

Childhood Hemiplegia

This is caused by brain damage as a result of haemorrhages in the brain just before birth, at birth or in the first few years of

CO-ORDINATION CONDITIONS

Dyspraxia (also known as Developmental Dyspraxia, sensory integration problems, coordination difficulties and motor-learning problems): There are various forms, all of which relate to difficulties in motor planning and organisation. It can affect the ability to cope with sensory stimuli and perceptual difficulties and can affect speech, eye, limb, body, hand and finger movements.

Developmental Co-ordination Disorder (DCD)

Professional opinion differs as to whether Dyspraxia is a sub-group of DCD or whether DCD and Dyspraxia are the same condition.

life. Most of these children who have moderate to severe damage are likely to be affected by specific learning difficulties whilst those with mild damage are less likely to be affected by SpLD. There can be difficulties in any or all of the following: reading, spelling and arithmetic. Movement, behavioural, emotional and social skills difficulties may also be present.

Two-thirds of these children will be of normal intelligence, the other third are likely to be of less than normal intelligence. Skills relating to non-verbal skills are the most likely to be affected with language skills being preserved whilst visuospatial skills are lost to some extent. Thus similar difficulties as those found in NLD will also be present.

Meares-Irlen Syndrome
(also known as Scotopic Sensitivity Irlen Syndrome)
This is a perceptual dysfunction affecting reading and writing based activities as well as depth perception.

Non-Verbal Learning Deficit (NLD).
"This is associated with a deficiency of white matter in the brain. Such individuals have marked difficulties in the processing of visuospatial information" which will affect symbolic language, geometry, writing/layout, map reading, reading diagrams and the use of planning and organisational tools. (Martin Turner, Head of Psychology, Dyslexia Institute)

This term is being used in some quarters to include forms of Dyspraxia/DCD and Childhood Hemiplegia. For further information on this condition read "Syndrome of non-verbal learning disabilities" by Byron Rourke (ISBN 0898623782 published by Guilford Publications). Bryon Rourke is a neuropsychologist based in Canada.

Throughout this book reference is made to difficulties (e.g. spatial relationships) commonly found in those who have Developmental Dyspraxia. Those students who have Childhood Hemiplegia or Non-Verbal Learning Deficit are likely to have similar problems in using planning and organisational tools.

Metabolic Dysfunctioning
There are various forms of metabolic dysfunctioning which can affect behaviour; e.g.:
▸ thyroid conditions (which can causes a form of ADHD),
▸ conditions relating to trace elements such as zinc deficiency (which causes behavioural disturbances)
▸ Essential Fatty Acid (EFAs) metabolic dysfunctioning (which causes high distractibility and behavioural changes).
See Book I for details.

Tourette Syndrome (TS)
(Also known as Tourette's Disorder and Tourette's Syndrome, Gilles de le Tourette Syndrome.) Causes the presence of tics (involuntary movements and vocalisations). Co-morbidity (the presence of more than one condition) is a particular problem with TS; several conditions are likely to be present (particularly the SpLD Profile behavioural conditions).

CFS/ME
Chronic Fatigue Syndrome (CFS) also known as Post Viral Fatigue Syndrome (PVFS) and Myalgic Encephalomyelitis (ME). Some believe that CFS is an umbrella term with ME being a sub-group of it. In the USA the term CFIDS is used. It is an illness characterised by fatigue, muscle pain and flu-like symptoms occurring after little or no mental/physical effort. It is usually a long term illness which can last for several years. Children (from as young as five years) and adults can have this condition. It causes changes in the brain chemistry which result in the person developing an acquired form of the Specific Learning Difficulty Profile. For more information on this condition see:
▸ Action for ME, Tel: 01749 670799,
▸ *A report of the CFS/ME Working Group* published by the government's Chief Medical Officer in January 2002 (available from the Department of Health, Tel: 0207 9724042).

Chapter I
Tourette Syndrome

Tourette Syndrome (TS) Also known as Tourette's Disorder and Tourette's Syndrome, Gilles de le Tourette Syndrome (after whom the syndrome was named). TS is an inherited neurological condition linked with chromosome 8. It is characterised by multiple involuntary motor tics and one or more involuntary vocal tics which occur by age eighteen years.[1] These two types of tics may or may not appear together. They will occur many times a day and this will last for longer than one year - during this time there is never a tic-free period lasting more than three consecutive months. The tics are not due to other causes such as other medical conditions; e.g. Huntington's disease or substances such as stimulants. There is believed to be a sub-group of TS who have PANDAS (Paediatric Autoimmune Neuropsychiatric Disorders Associated with Streptococcal infections) see page 4 and Chapter 7.

TS is more common in males than in females. Individuals can show two types of tics both of which are not under the control of the individual; i.e. body movements and vocalisations (where the individual makes noises or says words). The symptoms change over time. At the start the tics are simple; e.g. simple movements such as eye blinking, eye rolling, head shaking, nose twitching. The individual then progresses to more complex movements such as facial grimacing and movements which involve more body parts; e.g. kicking, body rocking, jumping, and turning. In most cases the symptoms lessen during adolescence and adulthood, in some they disappear entirely (usually by early adulthood) whilst for a few the symptoms may worsen in adulthood. Some individuals may have a mild version of this condition, a few will have a severe form of it so the number and intensity of tics can vary from small tics and noises to extreme shouting and swearing. Sometimes the number of the tics can be reduced if the individual is involved in another activity that is very pleasurable; e.g. chewing gum/sweets. The distress and impairment caused by the condition will affect important areas of functioning; e.g. learning, social life and career. There is no cure for TS but medication may help reduce the number of tics and in the future antibiotics may help the PANDAS group (see page 4).

Vocalisations

The vocalisations, which are a feature of TS, may start as squeaks, grunts, coughing, throat clearing etc. and go on to saying words or phrases. The words spoken may be the ones that the individual is thinking of but knows are totally inappropriate to say in a given situation but, despite making a huge effort not to say the words, they still are spoken. Individuals may repeat the words just spoken by

Incidence

It is believed that 1-2% of the child population have a type of tic disorder. Figures for adults vary between 1 in 2000[2] and 1 5000[3].

The various Tic Disorders are: identified by the length of the time that the tics have been present, the types of tics that occur and by the age at which the tics first started; e.g.

» Transient Tic Disorder (motor and/or vocal tics which last for between one to twelve consecutive months),

» Tic Disorder Not Otherwise Specified (tics last less than one month and start at age nineteen years or older.)

» Tourette Syndrome (referred to in the DSM –IV-TR criteria as Tourette's Disorder).

Footnote

1. There are rare cases where onset of TS occurs after eighteen years - see *Guide to Diagnosis and Treatment of Tourette Syndrome* by Drs. R Bruun, D. Cohen, J. Leckman at w.tourettesyndrome.org/page14.html).

2. See *Diagnostic and Statistical Manual of Mental Disorders, Fourth Edition, Text Revision.* Copyright 2000 American Psychiatric Association.

3. See *Tourette Syndrome: Myths and Facts* by Dr. Roger Freeman at www.tourette.ca/articles/ article2.html)

someone else or repeat other people's actions (including making obscene gestures). In about 10% of the cases the individual will make obscene vocalisations (called Coprolalia). These are distressing for the TS individual and for the listener, especially as such tics can develop in the primary school child who is then very embarrassed about his/her outbursts. The more severe the tics are, the more likely it is that the individual will find it difficult to relax, have low self-esteem and will lack confidence. Not surprisingly, such students can be under a great deal of stress which in turn can increase the number and severity of the tics. An example of a severe form of vocalisations can be seen in the Case Study Louise on pages 50-51.

Co-morbidity

Co-morbidity (more than one condition seen in the same person) is a particular problem when TS is present. As the case studies in this chapter, Chapters 6-7 and page 71 show, Autistic Spectrum Disorder and Obsessive Compulsive Disorder (page 71) are commonly associated with TS. At least half of those with TS will have ADHD, with the latter often appearing first. The more conditions that are present (and the more severe they are) the greater the impact upon the lives of individuals and their families. The areas of difficulty that are seen alongside TS are as follows:

- ➤➤ Difficulties associated with language impairment/auditory processing difficulties. See Books 3 and 4.
- ➤➤ Difficulties associated with the presence of Developmental Dyspraxia/ DCD; e.g. sensory-integration and sensitivity difficulties (including over-/under-reaction to sound, pain/touch sensitivity); poor gross motor skills (limbs, body), poor visual motor processing (may impair handwriting and other activities involving hand–eye coordination); poor fine motor skills (e.g. Verbal Dyspraxia, Oral Dyspraxia, Occulomotor Dyspraxia, Graphomotor Dyspraxia) developmental delays such as toilet-training (especially at night). See Book 6.
- ➤➤ Difficulties associated with Attention Deficits; for example, difficulties in timed tests, problems with memory and concentration, distractibility, impulsivity and hyperactivity.
- ➤➤ Emotional and behavioural difficulties: e.g. anxiety (in particular, severe separation anxiety), anger management difficulties, sleep problems, mood swings, depression (see page 10), emotional and social immaturity, school phobia, low self-esteem.
- ➤➤ Difficulties associated with learning; e.g., delayed skill acquisition or difficulties with handwriting/spelling and written expressive language, difficulties with mathematical calculations (though not necessarily mathematical concept difficulties) and poor organisational skills. See Book 3, *Literacy Solutions, Mathematics Solutions - An Introduction to Dyscalculia* and *Planning and Organisation Solutions* all by Jan Poustie.
- ➤➤ Difficulties associated with the presence of Autistic Spectrum Disorder (also known as Pervasive Developmental Disorder).

Children who have TS and ADHD (with or without a form of autistic spectrum disorder) are especially vulnerable to serious long-term educational impairment.

Adolescents find that the situation worsens with the tics increasing in severity which can make the teenage years particularly difficult for these students. Some may find that after puberty the tics reduce (and in some cases may virtually disappear altogether) - others are not so fortunate. Basically, the level (and range) of tics that are seen when the student is twenty-one years old are likely to remain for life. Students with the severe form can become very depressed about their condition and can become very tired because the number and severity of the tics use up so much of their energy and can even disrupt their sleep. Children and adults can become isolated and lonely, it can be especially difficult for them to establish intimate relationships because of the embarrassment caused by the tics. Career choices can also be limited because of the presence of the tics especially in those who are severely affected.

Adults
Individuals who have TS can become isolated, distressed and depressed in adulthood if adequate provision is not made.

Case study:
John

(Age 12 years, he has Tourette Syndrome, Asperger's Syndrome, OCD, ADHD.) His constant obsessive thoughts result in him not letting his mum go anywhere without him as he fears that she will die.

'I'm not a medical professional and I can't argue with 2 [sets of] diagnoses but all I see is a rude and naughty boy and that's what I'm going to deal with.'

It is comments like that above, made by a primary school teacher (in front of the head teacher of the school) to a parent of John, that makes one ashamed to be part of the educational system of this country. (For the rest of this case study see page 71.)

Family life
The presence of Tourette Syndrome can have a devastating affect on family life as parents and other relatives may find it very difficult to cope with the tics either in the home or in day to day social outings such as shopping and visiting relatives. The condition (especially in its severe form) requires great understanding on the part of all of the professionals involved and on the part of the classmates or work colleagues of the adult who has TS.

The problems faced by student and family

The following case studies and Case study Richard (page 48) highlight the problems faced by the child and family members (the names used are those chosen by the children). Referral for TS is via the GP but both they, and other medical professionals, can find themselves totally out of their league as DJ's case (below) and Louise's case (see Chapter 7) show. A number of medical professionals can become involved; e.g. psychiatrists, psychologists and psychotherapists (see pages 47, 71). Each will look at the same situation from a different perspective (which is not always helpful as DJ's case study shows). All education staff (including teaching assistants and dinner ladies) should be provided with appropriate training so that they can support the student and take proactive steps to avoid him/her being bullied and teased. Educators, such as the one in John's case study (left-hand column), display their ignorance of TS and lack of care. They cause great distress to parents (who are already stretched to their limits by the care needs imposed upon them by their child's conditions) and do nothing to help the child. Such educators need to attend the yearly meeting of the Tourette Syndrome (UK) Association to meet with the doctors, children and their parents and the adults who have TS. Then they can gain a true understanding of this condition.

Case study: DJ
DJ has TS, autism, ADHD and OCD.
<u>Granny view</u>: She is angry that her daughter took her grandson to the doctor, advised the GP of the grandson's habits and was told to just *'Go away'*. By now two GP's had said to them that the lad would grow out of them – *'It's a boy thing'*. The parents and grandparents then told DJ not to do the behaviours and so compounded the problem. Teachers spotted the tics and spotted children teasing him and felt he was *'taking the micky-taking on the chin'* so it was okay and so they only informed parents/grandparents of the situation once the lad had broken down. At 11 years old DJ was diagnosed with TS but the child psychiatrist who diagnosed it did not tell the family of the help and support group Tourette Syndrome (UK) Association.
<u>DJ's view</u>: '
> *I was upset that I could have it for the rest of my life and I was getting quite scared about the kids making fun of me as well. The most important thing that has made the difference since I was diagnosed was the teachers telling the kids at school about Tourettes.'*

<u>Mum's reaction to the diagnosis</u>:
> *'Guilt and bereavement for what was going to be.'*

This is a common reaction. Family members feel bereaved because the child they thought they had, no longer exists and so the child's future (and his family's) will be fundamentally different.
<u>DJ's starts secondary school.</u>
Prior to attending the school the psychiatrist sent a letter to the school

and the parents wrote a letter too. Mum also spoke to the form teacher the day before DJ started school and he said he would keep an eye on DJ. He came home from his first day at secondary school devastated, the other pupils had been verbally bullying him. Mum spoke to DJ, and the teacher had not appeared to have kept an eye on him at all. She spoke to the teacher that night and he was very apologetic. Mum advised school of the need for a meeting with the head teacher and form teacher and that DJ would not be returning to school until the meeting took place. The meeting was held the following week and included the school nurse (who had been in touch with the Tourette Syndrome (UK) Association) and the SENCO. During the hour's discussion they were 'fantastic' they said they wanted to learn how to help DJ. Strategies in use now are that DJ goes out of the room when he has a tic episode and returns once it has ceased. This means he needs a 'buddy system' so that when he returns after a tic episode (or after visits to see the clinical psychiatrist and psychotherapist) his buddy will explain the work that has been covered and what his homework is. He also needs a 'note taker' to take down the notes he misses. None of the family members are very impressed with one of the medical practitioners that DJ sees – but they were unaware that they could refuse medical treatment and ask for a different professional.

DJ's Mum:
> DJ was seeing a child psychiatrist (for the TS) and a child psychologist (for the OCD). For the 45 minutes that DJ saw the latter he managed to control his tics (even though this put him under great strain to do so which resulted in an increase in tics for the rest of the day). The child psychologist said to DJ, 'If you can control your tics here why can't you do it at home - are you trying to punish your family?'

It is this ignorance of TS on the part of some medical professionals that causes so much stress and distress to those who have TS (and their families). DJ's mum is a single mum and all the child psychologist appeared to be interested in was why DJ's father was not around.

Case Study: Yeti-man
Yeti-man has TS, autism, ADHD and OCD. He has had a statement since July 2002 and in September 2002 he started at a special school. He has physical tics. His greatest problem is in concentrating rather than the tics. The thing that upsets him the most is compulsive obsessive thoughts – he calls it 'his little man who bullies him'. He has a psychologist who is using cognitive therapy to help him reduce this behaviour. At age 6 years mum took him to the GP who thought he was autistic. An IQ test was administered and it was determined that Yeti-man was Moderate Learning Disabled (MLD) and not autistic. There was no extra assistance at school even though it became clear that he was struggling. Later he was diagnosed as having TS and ADHD. A house move took the family to a different Local Education Authority (LEA). At age 11 years Yeti-man saw another consultant psychologist

PANDAS (Paediatric Autoimmune Neuropsychiatric Disorders Associated with Streptococcal infections)
There is some evidence that PANDAS are implicated in the onset (and worsening) of TS in some people (see Chapter 7. Currently there are studies being undertaken to test this hypothesis. The Tourette Syndrome Association (TSA) of the United States (www.tsa-usa.org) are sponsoring a study in the UK to see if patients with TS have repeated streptococcal throat infections. This study is important as it is trying to establish whether or not a subgroup of subjects with TS have PANDAS. This would have major implications for our understanding of TS and will have possible treatment implications. If PANDAS , and a subset of patients with TS, occur as a consequence to streptococcal infection, then early treatment with antibiotics and antibiotic prophylaxis may reduce the severity, cure or even prevent TS.

Medication: Various forms of medication are available which help to reduce the incidence of the tics (e.g. Clonidine, Pimozide and Haloperidol) and the behaviours associated with OCD, see www.mentalhealth.com/book/p40-gtor.html

Assessment For details of how assessments are conducted, including the various rating scales that can be used, see: www.education.ucsb.edu/jimerson/tour.html/#as

Further information on TS: See websites mentioned in this book, Chapter 7, Appendix 5 and www.tourettesyndrome.net/chapters.htm and Great Ormond Street Hospital website: www.ich.ucl.ac.uk/factsheets/services/gosh_tourettes/tourettes2.html

Identification Solutions for Behaviour by Jan Poustie   ISBN 1 901544 82 6

INFORMATION
Tourette Syndrome UK Association
PO Box 26149, Dunfermline, Fife
KY12 9YU Helpline 0845 458
1252, Admin 01383 629600 Website:
http://www.tsa.org.uk/ Email:
enquiries@tsa.org.uk Has Family
Networking Contacts, free leaflets,
books/booklets and a website forum
for those who have an interest in TS.

Sunrise Tourette e-mail forum
Contains many carers who can offer
practical advice. E-mail the moderator
at sunrise@igc.org stating briefly why
you wish to join (it's a closed list by
invitation only).

db@educationsupport.fsnet.co.uk
David Bowles has TS. He (through his
consultancy, Education Support)
provides e-mail support for families
coping with Tourette Syndrome and
other neuro-behavioral issues.

Guidelines for educators
www.vh.org/Patients/IHB/Psych/
Tourette/Modifications.html#6 has
information on: Material Presentation,
Classroom Environment, Time
Management/Transitions, Mathematics,
Grading and Tests, Behaviour,
Reading, Organization and Handwriting

Books
📖 *Tic Attack;* children explaining what
it is like to have Tourettes.
📖 *My God, and Tourettes too!* An
autobiography by R F Oliver.
📖 *Tourette Syndrome – A Practical
Guide for Teachers, Parents and
Carers* by Amber Carroll and
Mary Robertson.
📖 *Tourette Syndrome - The Facts* by
Mary Robertson and Simon Baron-
Cohen
📖 *Making Allowances - personal
accounts of Tourette Syndrome*
compiled by Chris Mansley.
📖 *Tourette Syndrome and Repeated
Anger Generated Episodes* by Cathy
Budman M.D. and Ruth D Brunn
M.D. (pub. Tourette Syndrome
Association Inc, USA: also at web
site http://www.tsa-usa.org

who said that he definitely has autism but much to the parent's
surprise he did not appear to know of the commonly known link
between aggressive behaviour and TS. This resulted in the parents
losing their confidence in him and so they have not returned for a
further consultation. Yeti-man was then assessed at The National
Hospital for Neurological Diseases, Queen's Square, London where
both the autism and the TS diagnoses were confirmed.

Yeti-man's views:
> 'My name is .... I am twelve years old. Having TS is an advantage as
> we don't have to pay for parking because I'm disabled. I get tired from
> all the moving I do.'

Mum's comments:
> 'I took a book on TS into the school which they put on file but did not
> appear to read. I now highlight information so that they know which bits
> are relevant to him. Some educators cannot believe that his impulsive
> behaviour is not sheer naughtiness. There is a lack of awareness of the
> condition, the two headmasters we had before the special school were
> sensitive but one didn't pass the information on to the rest of the school.
> Information needs to be disseminated to everyone in the school -
> educators and non-educators alike. The social life of the family is very
> severely affected, its hard on the marriage and siblings. We are trying to
> obtain some residential care. Holidays are the biggest problem because
> we can't take Yeti-man's younger brother out. We are in the autistic
> society and every month they have a sibling group local to us which is
> run by the Child and Adolescence mental health service..'

8 year old brother's comments:
> 'Going out on an outing, going to the cinema is a bit hard. There are
> loads of small kids there and its like – it's a bit like having a younger
> brother. When Yeti-man comes to my school me and my friend hide in
> the toilets because we are embarrassed.'

Conclusion
A TS diagnosis can be a frightening prospect, many may feel that
the whole of life will be a disaster but that does not have to be the
case; adults can, and do, go on to succeed and lead fulfilled lives.
Early diagnosis, understanding, acceptance, respect and appropriate
support are key factors if TS individuals are to prosper but, as the
case studies show, such provision does not always occur. At the
2003 Annual Meeting of the Tourette Syndrome UK Association
families and adults shared with the authoress their experiences (for
good and ill) so that she could gain a greater understanding of the
impact of TS upon their lives. They did so with dignity, just wanting
her to listen. They did so with courage, ignoring their own
embarrassment at their child's behaviour, or their own tics. They
wanted their voice to be heard (hence the detailed case studies in
chapters 1 and 7). TS does have a major impact upon the life of
individuals (and their families) but, with the right support, that
impact can be lessened and a brighter future obtained.

CHAPTER 2
Understanding Attention Deficit behaviours
This chapter includes extracts from the ADHD Family Support Group UK pack [1] *The preferred term in the UK is Attention Deficit Hyperactivity Disorder (ADHD); however, it is possible that in the future the term 'Attention Deficits' will be used instead. Currently the term Attention Deficit Disorder and its abbreviation ADD are also in use in the UK. In this chapter the abbreviation ADHD has been used throughout, including quotes from authors who have previously used the abbreviation ADD.*

References and footnotes
See end of Chapter 3.

Attention Deficits can cause students to have major difficulties in functioning within the classroom and in achieving tasks that require mental effort. ADHD is a condition 'where the child/adult (in comparison to most children/adults of the same age and sex) has a markedly reduced ability to:

1.   maintain attention (i.e. poor concentration); [2]
2.   control words and deeds by thinking first (i.e. acting on impulse too often);
3.   regulate the amount of physical activity according to the situation (i.e. hyperactivity); [3]
4.   be motivated to listen to those in authority and to act on what he/she has been told.' [4]

Although it is believed that more boys than girls have this condition, it may be that we are not identifying the 'daydreaming' girls.' A school class of 20–30 children might expect to have one ADHD sufferer. It is three times more common in boys than in girls. There is increasing evidence that adults also can have their lives disrupted by ADHD.' [5] It is now believed that 'ADHD may be a lifelong disorder requiring lifelong assistance. The child, the family and the ADHD adult need continued support and understanding.' [6]

The history of ADHD
Although the condition has been recognised for some time in other countries such as the USA and Australia, professionals in the UK have been slow to recognise ADHD. 'In the 1960s, British child psychiatry assumed that this condition was rare and only occurred in children with obvious brain damage (such as those affected by meningitis, birth trauma, infection and epilepsy). In the 1980s university-based child psychiatrists in Britain accepted that the American view is correct. Unfortunately, hundreds of British child psychiatrists and general practitioners have passed through medical and postgraduate training without learning about the existence of ADHD and its treatment.' [7]

A school class of 20–30 children might expect to have one ADHD child. There are three main types:
1. Those who are mainly hyperactive.
2. Those who mainly inattentive,
3. Those who are a combination of inattentive and hyperactive. (This is the most common form.)
It is a neurobiological disorder caused by an imbalance of some of the neurotransmitters found in the brain. However, ADHD is only one of the causes of attention deficit behaviours.

Some of those with Attention Deficit Disorder are not hyperactive at all, they are the daydreamers gently dreaming their days away or escaping into daydreams when a task (or the stress of coping with an inappropriate provision) becomes overwhelming. Undifferentiated Attention Deficit Disorder refers to those children who exhibit disturbances in which the primary characteristic is significant inattentiveness without signs (or showing few signs) of hyperactivity. Recent studies of this group of ADHD students indicate that they tend to show more signs of anxiety and learning problems and qualitatively different inattention. They may have different outcomes than the hyperactive group.

The various forms of Metabolic dysfunctioning/trace element deficiency can also cause ADHD behaviours; e.g. thyroid dysfunction, Essential Fatty Acid (EFA) metabolic dysfunctioning and (also commonly seen alongside Dyspraxia) zinc deficiency. Certain food additives such as Aspartame are also believed to do this too. See Book 1 for details.

Co-morbidity and different forms of ADHD

ADHD is commonly seen alongside (co-morbid with) a number of conditions such as Dyslexia, Dyscalculia, Dyspraxia and ASD. Co-morbidity can cause students to have such a complex profile that the professionals may have difficulty in recognising that ADHD is present, especially if one of the lesser known forms is present; for example:

1. Undifferentiated Attention Deficit Disorder (UADD) is usually a non-hyperactive form. The person is a daydreamer and usually shows signs of anxiety; sometimes restlessness and fidgeting also occur.

2. In the 'Not as Specified' (NOS) form of Attention Deficits the student meets most, but not all, of the criteria for ADHD. Since there is no diagnosis of ADHD or UADD, such students may receive no provision. Dr Christopher Green (a leading figure in the management of those who have ADHD) has stated that even if all the criteria for ADHD are not met, such students may still need help and support to obtain their goals.

3. The student's hyperactivity (ADHD) takes a subtle form. S/he fidgets (for example, with fingers/hair), is restless and may talk 'too much'.

Causes of ADHD

'Over the years the presence of ADHD has been weakly associated with a variety of conditions including prenatal and/or perinatal trauma, and maturational delay. Such conditions are found in some individuals with ADHD; however, in most cases there is no history of any of the above.' [8] During recent years, the world of SpLD has become more complex and it now appears that we have two categories of Attention Deficit behaviours.

Category 1: ADHD behaviours caused by non-medical factors
This should be investigated first, as the student's behaviour can be dramatically improved by simple measures that are within the ability of the school/parents to achieve.

Category 2: ADHD caused by medical conditions
These may be a developmental condition, a food/chemical intolerance, an infection or metabolic dysfunctioning. (A combination of educational and medical interventions is required to improve the situation.)

1. ADHD behaviours caused by non-medical factors
Any (or all of these) can be present in a student exhibiting Attention Deficit behaviours and they can coexist alongside a medical condition causing a Category-2 form of ADHD.

a)   Intellectually superior (gifted) students
These can appear to show behaviours similar to those of the ADHD student. Parents may be more aware than educators that the student is

gifted for the student may hide his/her gifts in the school situation in an attempt to appear 'normal' in the eyes of his/her peers or the presence of the SpLD Profile conditions may mask the signs of giftedness. It may also be that his/her areas of giftedness do not fall within the curriculum level/areas being taught; for example the student may be gifted in science and so be able to understand scientific work five or more years above the level of the work done in the classroom (see Book 2).

b) Not eating enough or failing to eat the right foods
There can be various reasons for this; for example,

    1. If the lunch box consists of sweet and fatty foods and few starches (such as bread) the behaviour may deteriorate during the day (also see Book 1 on metabolic dysfunctioning).

    2. Some may eat no breakfast and so have concentration difficulties as soon as they get into school.

This poor diet can occur amongst all socio-economic groups! An unbalanced sugar level can occur. The student has 'sugar highs' just after taking sugar-laden foods (sweets and such like), then does not eat enough or does not eat mixed carbohydrate foods and so hits a 'sugar low'. Very uneven behaviours can result from this.

c) Not drinking enough
This results in irritability, difficulties in concentrating and headaches. Accessing enough liquid during the day can be difficult for a variety of reasons, as follows:

    1. Not all schools have working water fountains and for many primary school children the drink of milk at morning break is now a thing of the past.

    2. The commercialisation of school dining facilities (especially in the secondary sector) means that water may not be readily available. In the past, all school dinner tables had a large jug of water on them and all students drank water with their dinner.

    3. Now, in many schools, students are encouraged to buy manufactured drinks including cola rather than drink water. Unfortunately, cola (like tea and coffee) contains caffeine which further dehydrates the body rather than rehydrating it.

    4. The toilets (and the bullying that can occur within them) can be so appalling that some children choose to be thirsty all day, and have no drinks at all, just to avoid using them.

Of course dehydration does not just affect the students; it may also affect the educators too! Only those people who have very pale yellow urine are drinking enough water.

d) Mismanagement of the student because of the use of inappropriate behavioural management techniques
The truth is not always pleasant and so some people fail to

The student may manipulate his/her diet, not eating breakfast then eating caffeine laden snacks from the school's vending machines throughout the day so maintaining a continuous 'caffeine high' throughout the day. Both chocolate and cola drinks contain caffeine (as do some medicines such as cold remedies and vitamins).

In the ADHD child, temper tantrums can be particularly severe and carry on for many years. Normal measures to avoid/reduce such tantrums, such as distraction, may be ineffective. It is thought by some that these may evolve into panic attacks in the late teens/ adulthood. Such students need to interact with calming, soothing and reassuring adults.

Attention Deficit Disorder can be very destructive to learning and studying. The authoress is typical of those who have a form of attention deficit disorder. Trying to do ten things at once, her mind full of ideas, her desk in chaos. No sense of time so yes she will try to cram six months work into two weeks and then feel defeated when it just cannot happen. No wonder our students hand in their assignments late – of course there is time to go out and socialise; after all the assignment will only take an hour to do! Thus many of us burn the 'midnight oil' in order to have a chance of completing our work.

In school the child may be made to 'stay in' during breaks in order to get work done. This should not be done as it causes the child more stress and does not enable him/her to have the break from the classroom that s/he so desperately needs.

B/G-steem ISBN 1 873942354, published by Lucky Duck Publishing Ltd (Tel: 01179732881, www.luckyduck.co.uk) is a useful and easy to use self-esteem scale and locus of control scale (for 6-14 years). It identifies students with poor self-concept. Lucky Duck Publishing specialises in publishing books relating to behavioural issues.

acknowledge that some adults (both educators and parents) are inconsistent in their management of students and some even bully them. (In fact, some professionals bully other professionals and parents too.) A poor relationship between one teacher and the student can spill over into the rest of the child's interactions with adults within the school. (Note: It is easy for professionals to blame the parents for the child's behaviour but ADHD can make the best of parents look as though they lack good parenting skills.)

Once the student is given a bad name; s/he becomes only too easily 'blamed for everything' that happens in the classroom and punished for behaviours that would just receive a 'ticking off' if other children in the class do them. A vicious circle can set in. The student becomes anxious, which causes poor behaviours, which results in discipline, which causes anxiety, and so on. Some primary school educators are unaware that control strategies (such as sitting on the 'naughty chair/mat' and being kept in at playtime) are forms of public humiliation. The latter also results in the child having no chance of running off excess energy. Everyone can see these punishments (more so if the classroom looks out on to the playground).

The child may present a tough image but his/her self-esteem lowers each time such punishment is used, as would happen if an adult were publicly reprimanded in front of his/her peers. In desperation, the adult may send the student to another room. Any of these actions can result in the child's peer group/siblings copying the teacher's example and feeling that it is acceptable to reject or dominate (bully) the child. An alternative strategy is for the adult (in a non-heated moment) to discuss the situation with the student and decide upon a quiet place that the student moves to whenever his/her behaviour becomes unacceptable or s/he finds it difficult to concentrate on work. The emphasis should be on the student taking the initiative to go to the agreed location but, as a back-up, a discrete hand/verbal signal could be arranged whereby the teacher advises the student when the student's behaviour warrants such action.

e) Lack of opportunities to work off excess energy
This is due to lack of opportunities for physical exercise (and is of especial importance to boys who can have a great deal of excess energy). Few students walk to school nowadays, the days of daily PE sessions are long a thing of the past and many parents fear for the safety of their children if they go off to the park by themselves. The parents may not have the time (or may not wish) to accompany the child to the park themselves.

f) Unrealistic expectations of (and lack of acceptance of) normal childhood and teenage behaviour by adults

1. It is normal for children to be lively, demand attention, be

difficult and push the patience of adults in order to find their limits. In school, relatively few children will happily sit for long periods of time working at tasks that they find boring without misbehaving in some way.

2. Parents need to 'parent' and to accept that their children will impact on their daily lives.

Unfortunately, there is a risk that if the student manages to control most of his/her ADHD behaviours in the school setting (or has a non-hyperactive form, such as UADD) the professional may fail to realise that the condition is in fact present and will blame the student's behaviour on poor parenting! ADHD can make the best of teachers/parents look, and feel, totally inadequate.

2. ADHD caused by medical conditions
More than one form can be present; thus the student with the brain chemistry form of ADHD may have the behaviours worsened due to the presence of food intolerance/allergy.

A.   Brain chemistry as a cause of ADHD
Historically, the main cause of ADHD has been thought to be a chemical imbalance in the brain. Researchers looked at altered brain biochemistry as a cause of ADHD and they presumed 'differences in biochemistry as a cause of poor regulation of attention, impulsivity and motor activity. A landmark study by Dr Alan Zametkin and researchers at NIMH traced ADHD to a specific metabolic abnormality in the brain. Thus, it is now believed that ADHD is caused by a brain dysfunction. The brain relies on a number of chemicals, which it manufactures in order to enable us to:

- ▸▸ think clearly,
- ▸▸ feel reasonably stable in our mood,
- ▸▸ keep our fantasies and impulses under control,
- ▸▸ be satisfactorily motivated in life,
- ▸▸ regulate our energy output in proportion to the situation in which we find ourselves.

If a brain chemical is too concentrated, or insufficiently concentrated in an area of the brain, then brain dysfunction develops and the child (or adult) behaves in an abnormal way.' [10] 'The manufacture of the brain chemicals is controlled by the genes. There is considerable evidence that ADHD is a genetic disorder. [11] There is a likelihood that parents, siblings and other relatives of ADHD children will also have ADHD. Identical twins (having identical genes) are more likely both to have ADHD if one of them has ADHD than non-identical twins (who do not have identical genes). With this form of ADHD, a person's environment and/or life events may worsen or lessen its

Brain chemicals
An area of the frontal lobe of the brain which controls the ability to control oneself has been implicated in ADHD. Two chemicals are thought to be responsible for this brain dysfunction – noradrenaline (which keeps us alert) and dopamine (which dampens unwanted responses). 'In ADHD individuals there appears to be both a reduction and imbalance of these brain chemicals' [9] which is believed to occur in certain parts of the brain; e.g. the frontal lobe and the basal ganglia (see page 50).

Depression
This can occur when any of the conditions found in this book are present. Some anti-depressants work by increasing the available amounts of brain chemicals such as noradrenaline (also called norepinephrine in the USA) and Serotonin. The latter affects the way we feel, it relates to positive thought, adequate sleep and feelings of satisfaction, low levels are associated with depression. See *You mean I'm not lazy, stupid or crazy?! a self-help book for adults with Attention Deficit Disorder* by K. Kelly and P. Ramundo, pub. Scribner.

The fearful ADHD child may panic if his/her uniform/work is not perfect. S/he worries about breaking a school rule by accident and is fearful that s/he will not follow the teacher's instructions accurately. Such children find school highly stressful and their behaviour once in the car/at home can be horrendous to deal with.

Types of Attention Deficits

Individuals can have more than one form of ADD. Treatment and provision for the attention deficits is related to its causal factor/s. Thus we need a new way of classifying based on causal factor/s (each of which will have sub-groups as shown below); i.e.

Environmental ADD, e.g.:
» EFA Metabolic induced ADD (book 1)
» Allergy/intolerance induced ADD.
Structural ADD, e.g.:
» Cranial moulding induced ADD
Infection induced ADD, e.g.:
» Streptococcal infection induced ADD
All of the above will look like Classic ADD.
Classic ADD, e.g.:
» UADD, ADHD, ADHD-NOS.
Classic ADD is present if significant attention deficit behaviours remain once all the following factors have been removed from the equation by appropriate provision being made for the causal factor/s:
»   Items 1a-1f (pages 7-10),
»   Items B1-6 (page 11)
»   Diet and chemical allergy/ intolerance (pages 12-14).
The authoress believes that it is this group that are most likely to benefit from medications such as Ritalin.

The student who has attention deficits may interrupt others either verbally or physically, needing to be on the move or moving 'through their lips'.
Some can talk, and talk and talk and endlessly interrupt. (Oh, if only the listener realised just how many times they forced themselves not to interrupt and the stress it causes them to hold back.) As children we can drive carers and educators to distraction. Upon adulthood, life partners can suffer in a similar manner. Although 'ADHD usually begins between the ages of 3 and 4' [14] signs can be seen from birth onwards. 'If signs are noted before the child is two years old then the child is likely to have a more severe form of the condition.' [15]

manifestations, but environmental manipulations do not cure the disorder nor remove the symptoms.' [12, 13] Normally the cortex dampens the limbic system of the brain, which is closely involved in emotional behaviour. A chemical imbalance in the brain decreases the dampening effect of the cortex and causes difficulties in controlling actions and thoughts. Chemical interventions (such as Ritalin) may be used to regulate the neurotransmitters in the brain (e.g. dopamine) and so reduce unwanted behaviours and enable the individual to focus on academic work.

B. Other medically-based causes of ADHD
Nowadays, we realise that a much more complex picture exists and that we need to investigate the possibility of any of the factors below being present before we turn to chemical interventions.

1.   Food allergies/intolerances (see pages 12-13).
2.   Metabolic/thyroid dysfunction. Nutritional imbalances and some food colourings can have an impact on the function of the neurotransmitters of the brain (see Book 1).
3.   Environmentally-caused toxicity such as fetal alcohol syndrome, lead toxicity, chemical allergy/intolerance. (See pages 12-15,19, 32.)
4.   A lack of 'cranial moulding' during birth: the cranium (skull) consists of various bones, which at birth can move a small amount allowing cranial moulding to occur when the baby passes through the birth canal. If this moulding does not occur (for example, because of a very fast second stage of labour, a Caesarean birth) then ADHD behaviours can result. Such behaviours may be reduced through cranial osteopathy (available from specialist osteopaths) with older students being likely to require more sessions.
5.   Being a twin: twins (particularly boys) are especially likely to have difficulties in concentrating and staying on task. A contributing factor here may be that twins are often delivered by caesarean (see point 4 above). Less cranial moulding will occur during a vaginal birth because twin babies tend to have smaller heads in line with their lower birth weights. (See Help and Support List on page 63 for further information on twins.)
6.   The presence of another SpLD Profile condition which causes ADHD-like behaviours; for example, Receptive Language difficulties (see Book 3) and Auditory Processing Disorder (see Book 3) will cause such behaviours in a listening environment.

At what age will you see signs of ADHD?

ADHD can be VERY apparent by the time the child is two years old and for parents of such children the 'Terrible Twos' takes on a whole new meaning. For parents of severe ADHD children, acute social embarrassment starts here! Parents are unlikely to have any respite, for who will willingly take on their ADHD child for them? Baby-sitting circles are out as babysitters expect to look after sleeping children, not those who need little sleep or struggle to go to sleep. Young ADHD children may be building bird-tables at 9 o'clock at night and may not normally go to sleep until past 11pm! [16]

ADHD behaviours, diet and chemical allergy/intolerance
In the past, the view was held by many that 'certain foods, such as chocolate and cola drinks, can significantly worsen the ADHD symptoms but they do not cause the disorder'. [17] However, there is now a substantial body of knowledge indicating that there is a group of individuals in whom ADHD behaviours can be caused as a result of diet/chemical allergy/intolerance (and that such allergies/ intolerances may coexist alongside another form of ADHD.)

Hyperactivity
Hyperactivity was first described as a condition in 1947 in an article by Theron G. Randolph (in J. Pediat., 1947, 31:560–572) called *Allergy as a Causative Factor in Fatigue, Irritability and Behaviour Problems in Children*. Here children were described as being jittery, overactive, often aggressive, having temper tantrums, producing poor school work and sometimes being overweight. It is believed that ADHD behaviours can be reduced if certain foods, colourings or drinks are removed from the diet of those affected. Orange, wheat, chocolate and cow's milk are high on the list of common causes in the HACSG Database at the University of Surrey. (For details contact HACSG, Tel: 01243 551313.) Some people may be able to tolerate goat's milk. It is essential to take medical advice when modifying the diet (for example, when removing milk from the diet) as other sources of necessary nutrients (such as calcium) will need to be found. Some ADHD students eat only a small range of foods and may be very resistant to trying new foods/changing their routines. Interestingly enough, the authoress noted that, in one child, ADHD behaviours increased when she ate milk chocolate but were not increased when she ate white chocolate.

Chemical sensitivity

It has been realised since the early 1930s that some people have allergic reactions to some chemicals; for example, Dr Albert Rowe found that people could be allergic to fruit, including fruit from different plant families, such as apples and plums. Later research showed that commercial fruit had a different effect to fruit grown without chemicals, with people being able to eat the latter without showing signs of food allergy/intolerance. Of course, with our heavily-processed diet the number of chemicals added to our food during the second half of the twentieth century is extraordinary – believed to be over 3000! Even foods that we regard as 'natural',

Most parents will need advice (and some will need counselling) from professionals on how to deal with specific behaviours and habits, so that a home-management plan can be designed. Professionals must have a good understanding of ADHD: otherwise, the parents are likely to be blamed or at least to feel blamed, leading to needless guilt or accusation. [18] By recognising the disorder early and taking the appropriate steps to assist the ADHD child and family, many of the negatives commonly experienced by the child can be avoided or minimised so as to protect self-esteem and avoid a chronic pattern of frustration, discouragement and failure. [19]

The long-term cost is enormous, emotionally and financially, when needs not being met result in disaffected individuals. One father ,of an ADHD young man, estimated that the failure to meet his son's needs (which resulted in a one-way road to prison) has cost the country a million pounds. What better use we could find for such monies. How many students would be helped if we used this funding to prevent the damage being done in the first place by providing appropriately for these individuals, so enabling them to reach their potential so that they could lead successful and fulfilled lives?

Our fruit and vegetables are now sprayed many times before they reach our table. Although washing fruit does reduce some of the chemical load it does not remove it all. Many people are unaware that modern furnishings, and furniture itself, may slowly release huge numbers of chemicals into the air. This can be a particular problem in modern buildings (and especially in brand new ones) as they lack the draughts to air the rooms effectively. For some people, these chemicals result in food allergy/intolerance which leads to Attention Deficit/Hyperactive behaviours.

We know that there are many causes of attention deficit behaviours only one of which is ADHD and that various strategies can be used to reduce the behaviours. Ritalin (and other medications such as Concerta) will work for many (though not all) of the ADHD group of students. When these medications do work they are a blessing for all concerned: at last the student can function, at last the student can learn. For all students exhibiting attention deficit behaviours we need to look at factors within the environment which are impacting upon them so that we can make changes within the environment and so reduce the behaviours.

such as apples, may have been sprayed twelve times before they reach the vendor. Turning to organic foods can reduce the problem.

Diet and chemical allergy/intolerance
Theron Randolph and Ralph Moss in their book *Allergies, Your Hidden Enemy* (ISBN 0 7225 0981 2, Thorsons Publishers Ltd.) discuss several case studies of children with hyperactivity (with or without autism). They explain that, for these children, their unacceptable behaviours were very much reduced (or removed altogether) by removing chemical pollution such as gas fires and cookers and/or certain foods such as orange and particular types of sugar from the environment. For some, their food had to be chemical free, i.e. organic, for the symptoms not to return. (The highest grade of organic food in the UK is that which shows the Soil Association logo.) Thus, certain foods or additives may be triggering/worsening the student's behaviour. Brostoff and Gamlin note that the following physical indicators may then be present: muscle aches, stomach aches, rashes, headaches, bowel problems, pale or blotchy face and an intense thirst. It is important to remember that each of these physical indicators can also indicate other illnesses (for example, intense thirst is one of the indicators of diabetes) so one must look at physical indicators with care; it is unwise to ignore them. If parents have any concerns, they should talk to their GP.

The changing trend towards organic foods and 'green issues' has resulted in many people having a more informed and broader understanding of food intolerance/allergy. Sadly, not all professionals have moved in this direction. If the reader looks at the case study concerning Richard on pages 48-49, s/he will see that eventually he was diagnosed as having several SpLD Profile conditions. The mother had spent many years investigating his food intolerances and found that his behaviours were markedly reduced when his diet was changed.

Investigating food allergy/intolerance
In 1990 Brostof and Gamelin (in their book *Food Allergy and Intolerance*) advised parents who become heavily involved in seeking a food allergy/intolerance solution to be aware that some medical professionals who are sceptical of food intolerance may not believe the parent's observations. Such professionals might be on the look-out for Munchausen's Syndrome (also known as Meadow's Syndrome) in the parent. This was more likely to occur if the parent had emotional problems, appeared overprotective/anxious and seemed to be favouring lots of tests on the child. One wonders how much this still occurs today. A parent may also be viewed as being over-anxious etc. by the educational professionals from whom s/he is desperately trying to obtain an educational solution to his/her child's learning/behavioural difficulties.

Parents can become alienated from both medical and educational professionals, and very stressed, until adequate and appropriate provision is made for their children. Alcohol can also play a part in causing attention difficulties, see page 19 for further details.

<u>Environmental factors</u>
Sensitivity to the chemicals used in the environment, such as cleansers and/or the perfume/aftershave worn by adults and the materials used to construct the interior of the home/classroom and furniture can cause/ worsen difficult behaviours. When this occurs we may see a range of behaviours; e.g. excessive sleepiness, uncontrollable anger, mental confusion and hyperactivity. Such sensitivities can go hand-in-hand with food intolerances and sensory defensiveness (the latter student can find large rooms with poor acoustics difficult to cope with). We need to look out for behaviours being different in different environments including the different rooms within the school; for example, classroom, hall (with its specialist wooden floor polish) and dining room (bacterial cleansers). Modern classrooms contain plenty of writing implements that have a high chemical content; the air in classrooms where whiteboards are used rather than blackboards contain many such chemicals. Heating fuel can also cause behavioural difficulties, with cooking gas being implicated in various behavioural and physical difficulties. (Some people, such as those who have Dyspraxia/DCD or CFS/ME, can have an over-sensitivity to perfume/aftershave which causes them to find such scents very unpleasant and/or make them feel unwell. Close proximity to someone wearing these scents can cause the behaviour/concentration of the Dyspraxia/DCD student to deteriorate. HACSG have also noted that seasonal allergies (for example, to moulds and pollen) can also worsen behaviours. Windy days also cause much more lively behaviour in most children whether or not specific learning difficulties are present.

Attention deficits caused, or worsened, by the presence of streptococcal infection
See Chapter 7.

The problem of obtaining a diagnosis
The biggest problem with the recognition of ADHD has been that of accurate diagnosis. Many professionals are cautious about identifying a child as having ADHD because there is, as yet, no diagnostic test capable of recognising this condition. (At the moment, assessors determine the presence of ADHD through taking a case history, observation and through the use of tools such as the Conners' Behaviour Rating Scale.)

We have tests that can determine food intolerance/allergy, but many professionals have little knowledge of this area and so do not accept them. We lack tests for the metabolic dysfunctioning described in Book 1, though it is hoped that by 2005 such a test will exist. Some

Parents should seek medical advice when changing diet or when trying to determine the factors within the diet which are causing the problem. This is especially important if the child has already experienced any allergic reactions. Some children, such as those with asthma/nut allergy, experience life-threatening reactions when being tested for allergic reaction to some foods and so such testing must be conducted under medical supervision. For advice on allergy testing, either contact your local GP who may direct you to a local NHS centre or the British Allergy Foundation (for contact details see page 63).

MDF (commonly used instead of wood in DIY tasks) is known to release a large number of chemicals into the air. MDF can be sealed with a special sealant but that will wear off enabling the chemicals to go into the air.

Lead poisoning

This causes a wide range of behaviours including aggression and difficulties in maintaining concentration. The cause is lead in the environment; e.g. in
- paint especially in pre-1960 buildings,
- dust (e.g. when a building is being renovated, on working clothes when somebody is using lead either at work or because of a hobby),
- soil,
- water (through lead pipes in older buildings).
- air (e.g. if the person lives/works/ attends a school near a busy road).

Useful websites for further information:
- http://w.drgreene.com/21_153.html
- http://www.leadtest.co.uk/f.htm
- http://www.defra.gov.uk/ environment/chemicals/lead/ lead.htm

Eating, drinking and the rest of the world may not exist whilst the ADHD mind focuses totally on the task in hand. Fortunately, this exclusion of the rest of the world can be prevented by the use of an alarm to remind the person to eat when necessary and to break off work to communicate with their family/work colleagues.

professionals doubt a diagnosis of ADHD because of the difficulties of making an objective assessment. Many parents fear that any child who misbehaves will be inaccurately labelled as having this condition. For parents this fear is increased once they realise that, certainly in the USA and Australia, medication (in the form of drugs like Ritalin) is the favoured treatment. Often the child's behaviour is incorrectly attributed to poor parenting but, in fact, ADHD children can make good parents appear to be lacking in parenting skills. Coping with an ADHD child can be quite exhausting and the more members of the family who have the condition, the more difficult it can be for the family to function properly.

Reliable identification of ADHD

'The identification and diagnosis of children with ADHD is made easier by the provision of objective assessment provided by such professionals as teachers, social workers, health visitors etc..'[20] However, there is a small subgroup of ADHD children whose signs of ADHD are mainly apparent at home,[21] and so the parents' assessment also needs to be taken into consideration. 'The more domains assessed the greater certainty there can be of a comprehensive, valid and reliable diagnosis.'[22]

Overview of the treatment and provision for ADHD

It should be noted that both the non-medical and the medical forms of ADHD can be present in the same student and, in such cases, intervention should include both areas. All professionals need to be aware that parents have an important role to play in the management of ADHD. The child (unless attending a residential special school) is at home longer each day than he is at school. Therefore, it is the parents who have to cope with their child's ADHD the most. Social workers are trained to address and adjust interpersonal relationships and skills in the family. It is not an admission of failure to ask for their help, nor should parents be penalised for doing so. Some parents may prefer to use the services of charitable agencies such as Contact-a-Family (www.cafamily.org.uk) or the NSPCC instead. (Local contacts for each of these will be in the telephone directory.)

1. ADHD behaviours caused by non-medical factors:
The behaviours can be resolved or considerably reduced by appropriate modifications; for example:
A. enabling the student to obtain the drink/food s/he requires,
B. modifying the adult's behavioural-management strategies
C. providing a better match between the student and the curriculum level/areas studied. It should be noted that both gifted and ADHD students need the environment and the

task to be modified if they are to be anything other than 'square pegs in round holes'.

2. ADHD caused by medical conditions

A multi-modality approach to the treatment of ADHD is needed, with each of the different causal conditions requiring different groups of professionals to be involved. The aim with all groups of students is to assist the student medically, educationally, behaviourally (and, if appropriate, psychologically). Parents of ADHD children and adolescents play the key role of coordinating these services. Educators play an essential role in helping the ADHD child in the classroom. Adjustments in classroom procedures and work demands, sensitivity to self-esteem issues, and frequent parent–teacher contact can help a great deal.

Specific treatments for chemical imbalance of the brain

There are two main areas of treatment available in the UK: behavioural modification, and medication[24] to restore the brain's chemical balance via drugs such as Ritalin. Medication is not popular among UK professionals and there is a tendency of only parents of the more severe ADHD child tend favouring medication. Parents of children with low-level ADHD can sometimes cope by using alternative medicine such as homeopathy.[25] In the USA, coaching and counselling are also available.[26] Although the authoress provides ADHD coaching, there are, as yet, few practitioners of ADHD coaching in the UK. Best results are obtained when medical intervention, behavioural management programmes, educational interventions, parent training, and counselling (when needed), are used together to help the student reach his/her full potential and lead as normal a life as possible.

Outcome of ADHD

Now that we realise that there are several causes of ADHD, we need to accept that there will also be various outcomes according to the causal condition. Thus for those for whom a chemical intervention such as Ritalin is the solution, we are likely to find that their 'ADHD does not often occur in isolation from other psychiatric disorders[27] and many of this group of ADHD children will have co-existing oppositional and conduct disorders (see Table 2) with a smaller number (probably less than twenty-five per cent) having a learning disability.' [28] For those with a food/chemical intolerance/allergy or a metabolic dysfunctioning, once we remove the cause then the behaviour will change and successful learning can occur. For all of these students, various conditions within the SpLD Profile can also be present (see Table 4, page 25). In America, studies indicate that ADHD students have a far greater

'When drugs, such as Ritalin, are prescribed the professional team is likely to involve a psychiatrist, educational psychologist, teacher and/or support worker, a social worker, and the parents. Educational interventions such as compensatory educational instruction or placement in special education may also be required, depending upon the particular child's needs.'[23] Ideally, treatment should also include consideration of the individual's psychological adjustment; targeting problems involving self-esteem, anxiety and difficulties with family and peer interaction.

Those with ADHD are the 'all or nothing' people. One minute so intensely involved in something that nothing else gets a 'look-in', the next minute they are off - like an express train. They may learn to climb before they learn to walk. They may seem to run almost as soon as walking has been mastered. Not for them the fiddly things of life. Some students rush into writing a story/assignment (not worrying about planning it or writing it or spelling it). Other fret and become frustrated because the story they write is not as good as the one in their mind. Some students know that the story/assignment is in their mind so why should they go to all of that bother to show it to you by writing it down?

Identification Solutions for Behaviour by Jan Poustie   ISBN 1 901544 82 6

Bipolar disorder
(also known as manic depressive illness) For details of this condition see: http://www.nimh.nih.gov/publicat/bipolarmenu.cfm

Some of those with ADHD will also have Bipolar disorder. It is a brain disorder which causes dramatic (and extreme) mood swings. emotional highs and lows which affects both children and adults. People with Bipolar Disorder often have a thyroid condition too (see Book 1 of library - *The Specific Learning Difficulties Profile and Associated Conditions* by Jan Poustie).

likelihood of grade retention, school drop out, academic underachievement, and social and emotional adjustment difficulties. Most experts agree, however, that the risk of poor outcome of ADHD children and adolescents can be reduced through early identification and appropriate treatment and provision.

Adulthood

Compensation by the mature brain of adulthood and possibly the weakening influence of the ADHD genes do mean that only about 50% of ADHD children will have symptoms in adulthood. Work and lifestyle choices can help the ADHD adult get on in life with minimal difficulties. However, it is possible that adults who are still experiencing their ADHD may be more prone to depression and anxiety (see page 10). Adults with a childhood history of ADHD have more contact with the police and courts than those with no such history. Nevertheless, the vast majority of ADHD adults are not antisocial. [29]

The advantages of ADHD may not be seen until the end of the school years or adulthood. Thus the inaccurate/inappropriate focusing of attention of the young child, and the teenager, can be harnessed in later life to a depth and length of focus that leaves their peer group far behind. ADHD individuals may be like runaway wild horses but with the right support and the use of appropriate coaching and intervention strategies they can easily outdistance the rest of the field.

Examinations and ADHD

Attention Deficit students often lack the staying power for long-term in-depth revision (especially of subjects that they dislike). Such students may well need a sudden spurt at the last minute to achieve their goals. At GCSE level, they may only be able to do such a quantity of revision for the week prior to the exams and, if they are lucky, they will maintain it for another two weeks. However, their academic stamina may not last till the end of the GCSE period.

Case Study: Steven

Steven was taking a City and Guilds engineering course. Prior to entering college, it had been thought by Steven's school that he had slight literacy difficulties which were 'Dyslexic' in nature though Dyslexia itself had not been diagnosed. Steven received (from the age of sixteen) specialist tuition for one and a half years. It soon became apparent that he had considerable planning and organisational difficulties, did not pay attention to small details, had great difficulties in expressing himself when writing and his spelling was weak. He fitted the category of Attention Deficits NOS.

For the first year, Steven was taught as part of a small group where the concentration was on planning and organisational skills. He was taught Mind Mapping™ and much to the delight of his mother was

The goal with Attention Deficit students is like that of an Olympic athlete – to bring them to their peak on the day of the examination and not a day earlier or later. The tutor is often unsure as to whether s/he has got it right until the moment that s/he finds out the examination results – so such Attention Deficit coaching can be a very nerve-wracking experience.

then able to keep his bedroom tidy! Using a computer, he was taught to improve his writing by editing his text and adding in adverbs, adjectives and so forth. In the second year, he was given one-to-one tuition.

During the first term, the author concentrated on his English language skills. Steven had very low self-esteem because of his failure to achieve a pass at English GCSE. It was necessary to convince him that he was capable of GCSE-level work. During the second term, the focus moved to revision study skills. Various strategies were explored for learning, including colour-coding words, Mind Mapping, drawing illustrations and answering questions on the text. The third term concentrated on two areas, examination strategies and motivation. A revision timetable was designed with Steven, complete with a system of rewards that was appropriate for him.

To begin with, Steven was hopeless at keeping to his timetable. He was never criticised for this nor for forgetting to bring his work – a common failing for those who have Attention Deficits. Instead, either new ways of keeping to the timetable were discussed or a timetable designed with lower goals was made. Only when he could keep to the timetable successfully was his workload gradually increased.

Conclusion

ADHD does not generally have a good press. Many only see the poor behaviour that the individual may exhibit and do not realise that, like many of the other conditions within the SpLD Profile, ADHD gives the individual both strengths and weaknesses. Some individuals are able to exist on two to four hours sleep a night for several days/weeks and even months. The end result of such focusing for such exceptional lengths of time can be a huge amount of work achieved in a short time, with adults capable of working long hours (maybe as many as five or six without stopping).

Some individuals possess the ability to think on many planes simultaneously at speed. Once this ability is harnessed, the mind is enabled to process information very quickly and make connections between different strands of thought that others may not easily be able to achieve. The combination of unusual thinking skills and depth of focusing can be quite formidable, both in school and in the workplace.

Recommended publication

📖 *PRIM: Pre-Referral Intervention Manual* (available from ADDISS - see page 29) contains a wealth of excellent strategies for students with attention deficits. This is an excellent book full of strategies that can be used when attention deficit behaviours are present no matter what their cause.

Steven and examinations
Modifications in behaviour need to be rewarded on a very frequent basis. For some this may mean every few minutes. This can become a big problem when external examinations are being taken, as the individual can find it very difficult to put in some work now (e.g. assignment work) for an exam grade that will come later. During the month before the exam, Steven concentrated on doing past examination papers (both orally and in writing) and the questions were marked individually as pass, merit or fail. During this time, Steven realised that he would receive a pass for some of the questions and a fail for others. This spurred him on dramatically to increase the amount of revision done. He then 'peaked' at just the right time and achieved a credit in his external exam.

Information sources
www.nofas.org
An extremely useful site with plenty of information on FAS and how to help those affected by it. Also sells a number resources on FAS including: *Fetal Alcohol Syndrome: Practical Suggestions and Support for Families and Caregivers* by Kathleen Tavenner Mitchell, *The Challenge of Fetal Alcohol Syndrome:Overcoming Secondary Disabilities* edited by Ann Streissguth and Jonathan Kanter, *Fetal Alcohol Spectrum Disorder: A Video Overview*

www.rnw.nl
Type Fetal Alcohol Syndrome into this site's search engine and it will take you to a great deal of information on FAS.

NOFAS suggest a range of strategies that can help FAS children including:
▸ Giving the child choices and encourage decision-making.
▸ Focus on teaching daily living skills.
▸ Establish routines so that the child can predict coming events.
▸ Give the child lots of advance warning that an activity will soon change to another one.
▸ Break his/her work down into small pieces so that s/he does not feel overwhelmed.
▸ Be concrete when teaching a new concept. Show the student what to do.
▸ Have the child repeat back his/her understanding of your instructions.
These sensible strategies are also likely to benefit the majority of students who have the conditions found in this book.

Alcohol and attention difficulties

There is no known safe amount of alcohol for a pregnant woman to drink since all the alcohol passes into the baby's bloodstream. (Dr Ann Streissguth, Director of Fetal Alcohol and Drug Unit, Washington Medical School, Seattle, USA, at the www.nofas.org website). There are several conditions that can arise from the mother's drinking of alcohol:
▸ Alcohol-Related Neurodevelopmental Disorder (ARND) - functional or mental impairment due to prenatal alcohol exposure,
▸ Alcohol-Related Birth Defects (ARBD) - malformations in the skeletal and major organ systems.
▸ Fetal Alcohol Syndrome (FAS) - see below
Each results in neurological deficits which can cause a variety of difficulties; e.g.
▸ poor motor skills including poor hand-eye coordination.
▸ behavioural and learning problems, including difficulties with memory, attention and judgement.
Fetal Alcohol Syndrome (FAS) occurs in approximately 3 in a 1000 live births though there is evidence that 1 in 100 individuals are affected when we look at all of the different alcohol related neurodevelopmental conditions together. (The other conditions may be less easy to recognise since the facial abnormalities found in FAS are not present.) Early intervention is best. However the stigma attached to one's child having a condition that was caused by the parent has resulted in some medical professionals being reluctant to make diagnosis. Thus some individuals may not be diagnosed until late teens or adulthood by which time secondary disabilities such as dropping out of school and developing alcohol and drugs problems may have occurred. 'Research indicates that being raised in a stable, nurturing home environment and obtaining an early diagnosis for the child are strong "protective factors" that can contribute to a lower rate of secondary disabilities.' (Dr Ann Streissguth)

Fetal Alcohol Syndrome (FAS)

This results in a distinct pattern of minor facial abnormalities with short palpebral fissures (width of the eye slits) a smooth and/or elongated philtrum (the ridges that run between the nose and the lips) and a thin or smooth upper lip. Other symptoms include babies being born shorter or lighter, dysfunction/damage to the central nervous system, small head and brain, seizures, eye malformations and growth deficiency. Difficulties that can be seen as part of this condition are difficulties in memory, learning, attention (this is a serious problem), problem-solving and language development. Impulsive behaviour, poor money handling, poor comprehension, food intolerances and hearing problems can be present too. There are also likely to be problems with mental health and social interactions including difficulties in bonding to parents. FAS students are also likely to be naive.

CHAPTER 3
Identifying Attention Deficit Disorder

Section 1 consists of the DSM-IV diagnostic criteria, which are used by many professionals. Section II includes the criteria used by the AD/HD Family Support Group UK. Use the information in either Section 1 or the ADHD checklist in Appendix 1 as the basis for your referral. If the individual has less than the stated number of criteria; for example only four or five from either Section 1 or the checklist, then the NOS (Not Otherwise Specified) subgroup of Attention Deficits may be present and provision may still be required. Oppositional Defiant Disorder or Conduct Disorder (see page 65) may be seen alongside Attention Deficits. DSM-IV Diagnostic Criteria for ADHD and Oppositional Defiant Disorder below is reprinted with permission from the Diagnostic and Statistical Manual of Mental Disorders, Fourth Edition. Copyright American Psychiatric Association, pages 83–85, 78-83.

Section I

Table 1: Diagnostic Criteria for Attention-Deficit/ Hyperactivity Disorder

A. Either (1) or (2)

(1) six (or more) of the following symptoms of inattention have persisted for at least six months to a degree that is maladaptive and inconsistent with developmental level;
Inattention

  (a) Often fails to give close attention to details or makes careless mistakes in schoolwork, work or other activities.

  (b) Often has difficulty sustaining attention in tasks or play activities.

  (c) Often does not seem to listen when spoken to directly.

  (d) Often does not follow through on instructions and fails to finish schoolwork, chores or duties in the workplace (not due to oppositional behaviour or failure to understand instructions).

  (e) Often has difficulty organising tasks and activities.

  (f) Often avoids, dislikes or is reluctant to engage in tasks that require sustained mental effort (such as schoolwork or homework).

  (g) Often loses things necessary for tasks or activities (e.g., toys, school assignments, pencils, books, or tools).

  (h) Is often easily distracted by extraneous stimuli.

  (i) Is often forgetful in daily activities.

(2) six (or more) of the following symptoms of **hyperactivity-impulsivity** have persisted for at least six months to a degree that is maladaptive and inconsistent with developmental level.

Authoress' notes to ADHD criteria:

<u>Maladaptive</u> = individual's behaviour is inappropriate to the situation.

<u>Tasks involving mental effort:</u> the individual is likely to work better in a quiet environment. S/he may leave homework until the last minute and may need a parent for company.

<u>Losing things:</u> adults lose their keys, glasses, pen etc. (This is also associated with Dyslexia - Book 4 and Dyspraxia/DCD - Book 6.)

<u>Forgetfulness:</u> Individuals forget what they should be doing, where they should be going, etc.

<u>Difficulties in organising tasks and activities:</u> e.g. individuals cannot get organised in the morning for going to school. There are also various medical conditions where this difficulty can be present, including Autistic Spectrum Disorder (see Chapter 4).

<u>Appearing not to listen when spoken to:</u> this can be present as part of several other conditions (see Specific Language Impairment - Book 3, Auditory Processing Disorder – Book 3 and Autistic Spectrum Disorder – Chapter 4.)

<u>Not seeing the finer details of a task/activity:</u> individuals will make careless errors when doing academic tasks (e.g. reading, writing, spelling and numeracy), non-academic tasks and activities. This behaviour can occur because the individual deals with a task as a 'whole' and so does not see the 'parts' of the task clearly.

<u>Extraneous stimuli:</u> these are things outside of the individual that s/he hears, sees, smells and touches etc.

<u>Difficulties in sustaining attention:</u> the longer the task/activity, the greater the chance of losing concentration. More severe cases may show considerable difficulties in maintaining attention for even a few minutes. However, the individual may be able to concentrate for a very long time on a task/activity that is of interest to him/her and may become frustrated/angry if s/he has to leave the task/activity.

Authoress' notes to ADHD criteria:
If hyperactivity/impulsivity is present the following are also likely to be present:

▸▸ Frequent fidgeting, restlessness or impulsive behaviour.
Some individuals control it by making small, quiet movements which are not so noticeable to the teacher/parent.

▸▸ Often being 'on the go'.
This behaviour is very exhausting for the adult who has to cope with it. There are also various medical conditions that can cause such behaviour including Autistic Spectrum Disorder.

▸▸ Difficulties in waiting for his/her turn. Adults may hate waiting at the supermarket checkout, and so interrupt or intrude on others (is also associated with Specific Language Impairment, see Book 3).

Authoress' notes on diagnostic criteria for ADHD
The presence of 1c, 1e, 1g and 1i can put a great strain on other family members. If more than one member is affected, getting ready to go anywhere (for example, to school in the morning or on holiday) can be very stressful. The presence of 1a can result in the individual working very hard on an assignment/examination question. However, due to misreading the instructions/question and/or failing to realise that the work is incomplete, s/he gains a lower grade than is expected for his/her intelligence.

Hyperactivity
(a) Often fidgets with hands or feet or squirms in seat.
(b) Often leaves seat in classroom or in other situations in which remaining seated is expected.
(c) Often runs about or climbs excessively in situations in which it is inappropriate (in adolescents or adults, may be limited to subjective feelings of restlessness).
(d) Often has difficulty playing or engaging in leisure activities quietly.
(e) Is often 'on the go' or often acts as if 'driven by a motor'.
(f) Often talks excessively.

Impulsivity
(g) Often blurts out answers before questions have been completed.
(h) Often has difficulty awaiting turn.
(i) Often interrupts or intrudes on others (e.g, butts into conversations or games).

B. Some hyperactive – impulsive or inattentive symptoms that caused impairment were present before age 7 years.
C. Some impairment from the symptoms is present in two or more settings (e.g., at school [or work] and at home).
D. There must be clear evidence of clinically significant impairment in social academic or occupational functioning.
E. The symptoms do not occur exclusively during the course of a pervasive developmental disorder, schizophrenia, or other psychotic disorder and are not better accounted for by another mental disorder (such as Mood Disorder, Anxiety Disorder, Dissociative Disorder or a Personality Disorder).

Code based on type
314.01 Attention-Deficit/Hyperactivity Disorder, Combined Type:
If both Criterion A1 and A2 are met for the past 6 months.

314.00 Attention-Deficit/Hyperactivity Disorder, Predominantly Inattentive Type:
If Criterion A1 is met but Criterion A2 is not met for the past 6 months.

314.01 Attention-Deficit/Hyperactivity Disorder, Predominantly Hyperactive-Impulsive Type:
If Criterion A2 is met but Criterion A1 is not met for the past 6 months. Coding Note: for individuals (especially adolescents and adults) who currently have symptoms that no longer meet full criteria, "In Partial Remission" should be specified.

314.9 Attention-Deficit/Hyperactivity Disorder Not Otherwise Specified
This category is for disorders with prominent symptoms of inattention or hyperactivity-impulsivity that do not meet the criteria for Attention-Deficit/ Hyperactivity Disorder. Examples include:

1.   Individuals whose symptoms and impairment meet the criteria for Attention Deficit/Hyperactivity Disorder, Predominantly Inattentive Type but whose age at onset is 7 years or after.

2.   Individuals with clinically significant impairment who present with inattention and whose symptom pattern does not meet the full criteria for the disorder but have a behavioural pattern marked by sluggishness, daydreaming, and hypoactivity.

Table 2: Diagnostic Criteria for 313.81
Oppositional Defiant Disorder

A pattern of negativistic, hostile and defiant behaviour lasting at least six months, during which four (or more) of the following are present:

1.   Frequent loss of temper.
2.   Frequent arguments with adults.
3.   Frequent defiance of or refusal to comply with adult's requests or rules.
4.   Frequently annoying people on purpose.
5.   Frequently blaming others for his/her mistakes or misbehaviour.
6.   Frequently being touchy or easily annoyed by others.
7.   Frequently being angry and resentful.
8.   Frequently being spiteful or vindictive.

Note: Consider a criterion met only if the behaviour occurs more frequently than is typically observed in individuals of comparable age and developmental level.

(B)   The disturbance in behaviour causes clinically significant impairment in social, academic or occupational functioning.
(C)   The behaviours do not occur exclusively during the course of a psychotic or mood disorder.
(D)   Criteria are not met for conduct disorder, and, if the individual is 18 years or older, criteria are not met for antisocial personality disorder.

Reprinted with permission from the Diagnostic and Statistical Manual of Mental Disorders, 4th edition. © 1994, American Psychiatric Association, pp. 91-95

Section II

Table 3: Indicators of ADHD in the classroom
(Based on material supplied by ADHD Family Support Group UK.)

1.   The young child with ADHD is often an underachiever who seems to have more potential than s/he is actually using.
2.   The child's achievements often seem uneven, and seem to vary with the type of learning activity rather than the skills involved in the activity.

Authoress' notes to ODD criteria
At least five of these indicators should be present to a degree beyond what would normally be expected for his/her age group. Some children show few if any signs of this disorder at school but severe signs at home. Such children can become very resentful of school and educators.

Refuses/resists rules:
Such children can cause conflict in the home, as either a major confrontation has to take place to get them to do their share of household chores or else they are seen as 'getting away with it' by their brothers and sisters. This behaviour can be overcome to a certain extent if they have the adult with them when doing the task/obeying the rule.

Blames others:
For example, when the child knocks a drink off the table that s/he placed there, it is the parent's fault for bringing him/her the drink in the first place. Individuals with this disorder are exceptionally difficult to live with and the whole family can be under stress. Such children may be rarely invited away for a night, let alone a weekend, and so the parents often have very little respite.

(Also see Oppositional Defiant Disorder and Conduct Disorder - page 70.)

There is a positive side of ADHD
Some of you reading this will love the way that those with ADHD can think 'on the fly', the ideas we can come up with, the magnetic personality that may be present, the way we can learn so much if we are really interested in your subject.

Others of you reading this will find us a struggle to manage (at home, at work and in the classroom) and find us irritating, frustrating and stressful to deal with. The only way to get around our behaviours is through learning to understand us and help us to develop strategies to overcome the problems the conditions causes us.

3.   The child with ADHD may have learning problems similar to other children with Specific Learning Difficulties, such as Dyslexia.
4.   The child seems disorganised, forgetful, and messy with his or her materials.
5.   At times, the child with ADHD may persevere at an activity, or be very rigid in his/her approach to problem solving.
6.   The young child with ADHD is frequently fidgety when sitting and impulsive in behaviour. S/he jumps to respond without thinking through the answer. The hands (and bodies) of such individuals are always waving in the air.
7.   This type of child is very distractible and may have a short attention span compared to other children of the same age. Any little sound or minor movement nearby can be distracting to the child.
8.   Relationships with other peers may be quite poor, and the child with ADHD often has few, if any friends. Other children do not like the disruptive, fidgety, impulsive behaviour and the tantrums of this child, and therefore they often avoid him/her.
9.   Although this child is often unaware of the effect s/he has on others, s/he may avoid joining in group activities. The child with ADHD may appear socially withdrawn, shy and immature compared to peers.
10. Educators often describe the child with ADHD as one who needs, or benefits from, one-to-one instruction.

Any or all of the following indicators may be present, and many may still be present in adulthood though perhaps less apparent:

▸   easily bored;
▸   fails to complete routine jobs unless supervised;
▸   daydreaming;
▸   thinking on several different planes at once;
▸   seeing unusual connections between items of information
▸   there is some evidence that some individuals may have continence difficulties with bladder and/or bowel. (This appears to affect boys more than girls.) In such cases, it is likely to occur when under stress; soiling and smearing of the faeces have been known to occur;
▸   an inappropriate response to praise, perhaps reacting in a negative or angry way. Can regard praise as being patronising or even sarcastic;
▸   inability to work for bigger, more lasting rewards, preferring instead to work for immediate but smaller ones;

Ultimately, the child with ADHD often has problems with self-esteem and a negative attitude towards education in spite of apparent good intellectual potential and an emotionally healthy family situation.

▸ may lie to get what s/he wants or, more commonly to get out of trouble; the latter can be a sign of low self-esteem. Such individuals may seem to be extremely manipulative to others. The individual may have an extremely poor short-term memory difficulty, making it difficult for him/her to remember instructions for very long;

▸ needs a high level of stimulation;

▸ presence of 'Gilles de la Tourette Syndrome' (commonly known as Tourette Syndrome) may be present. This is characterised by the individual making repetitive and involuntary movements. Involuntary movements are ones over which an individual has no control. The person can also make involuntary vocal sounds (see pages iv, 1-5, and 50-51).

Other behaviours may also be seen alongside or as part of ADHD.

Both Conduct Disorder and Oppositional Defiant Disorder can be seen alongside ADHD. If a severe/ moderate form (or several) of any of the following indicators are seen then one needs to investigate the possibility of Conduct Disorder/Oppositional Defiant Disorder being present (see page 70).

▸ Refusal to submit to rules and requirements, though some of those who do not show noticeable signs of ADHD in the classroom are fearful of disobeying any school rules.

▸ Has difficulties in restraining his/her behaviour to fit the situation.

▸ Inflexibility and an unwillingness to compromise. Such children are very difficult to negotiate with, though if such a technique is used from toddlerhood, it is possible for them to learn this skill by about ten years of age. Some individuals carry this behaviour on into adulthood, which can make it very difficult to form lasting relationships);

▸ Being highly critical of others and verbally/physically bullying them;

▸ Severe temper tantrums. Can have a very quick temper that is lost over the slightest thing that annoys them.

▸ Too frequently not doing what has been requested. Can be difficult to control. Can be very aggressive or can get their own way by passively refusing and/or avoiding doing things.

▸ lack of regret over behaviour and/or refusal to accept that their behaviour was inappropriate/incorrect for the situation.

▸ may not respond to punishments of any kind.

Need for an 'emotional high'.
Usually we learn new skills through methods which involve visual/auditory and movement learning styles. However, some ADHD people seem to need an 'emotional high' where they, or those around them, become highly excited before the ADHD student can calm down, and settle down to achieve a task. Unfortunately, this all too often seems to involve the ADHD person in unwittingly stretching the patience of the educator/parent so far that they lose their temper. The ADHD person will then achieve the task. If this happens during the struggle to get the child to sleep at night the child may then fall asleep with ease, leaving an emotionally exhausted parent who may take hours to recover from the experience.

A student who 'plays the class clown' can be 'egged on' by his/her peer group because the resultant conflict between the student and the teacher provides entertainment for the rest of the class. The ADHD student can also become the focus of teasing/bullying by their classmates.

Some will watch the television no matter what programme is on. This trait can be used to an advantage in children by encouraging them to watch educational programmes and/or play good quality educational computer games. (For such children it may be best not to have any of the usual games on the computer as these are always likely to be the preferred choice.)

Table 4: Indicators which can be present in ADHD and/or other SpLD Profile conditions

▸▸ Fear of failure, being teased and/or ignored by their peers can cause the child to avoid school. This can occur via deliberate actions (for example, playing truant, refusing to leave home) and/or as a result of stress-related illness; for example, stomach pains, irritable bowel syndrome, headaches and feeling sick. (Can also occur with many of the other conditions found within the Profile such as Specific Language Impairment - Book 3, Dyslexia - Book 4 and Dyspraxia/DCD - Book 6.)

▸▸ May have low self-esteem and become severely depressed because they blame themselves for failing to achieve in behavioural and/or academic tasks. (See Dyslexia - Book 4, Dyspraxia/DCD - Book 6 and Asperger's syndrome - Chapter 6.)

▸▸ May play the part of the 'class clown'. If this occurs at a low level it may be accepted by the primary school teacher but by the time the child reaches secondary school it can easily become behaviour for which detentions are given (see Dyslexia - Book 4).

▸▸ Not remembering instructions (see Specific Language Impairment - Book 3).

▸▸ Is likely to underachieve academically unless appropriate provision is given (see Dyslexia - Book 4 and for numeracy difficulties – *Mathematics Solutions* pub. Next Generation).

▸▸ May have difficulties in starting tasks even if s/he wants to do something very much and/or may give up easily (for example, may give up playing a musical instrument very soon after starting to learn it). This behaviour can be because the individual has poor planning and organisational skills and so does not know where to start the task and/or be due to fear of failure (see Dyslexia – Book 4 and Dyspraxia/DCD – Book 6).

▸▸ May dislike being touched (see Dyspraxia/DCD – Book 6 and Autistic Spectrum Disorder – Chapter 4.)

▸▸ May like to watch a great deal of television, though some may never sit still long enough to watch it! Watching television seems to help some individuals relax and escape their stress. (Note: Individuals with certain types of Near-vision Dysfunctioning/Occulomotor Dyspraxia can find looking at a television screen/VDU less stressful than looking at anything else around them, especially if they are affected by difficulties in the ability to change focus. In severe cases, the child may need to learn to read using a computer-based method (see Book 3).

▸▸ May have very noticeable food fads and may eat only a few foods. The person can be very resistant to trying new foods. Some people seem to have difficulties in recognising the body's signals that they are hungry and/or are able to ignore such signs until they become severe when, even then, they may not realise what the stomach pains mean (see Autistic Spectrum Disorder – Chapter 4).

▸▸ May be clumsy (see Dyspraxia/DCD – Book 6, Autistic Spectrum Disorder – Chapter 4 and Asperger's Syndrome - Chapter 6).

▸▸ Writing difficulties may be present (see Book 6)

▸▸ DAMP syndrome may be present. This is a combination of deficits in attention, motor control and perception. (See Autistic Spectrum Disorder - Chapter 4 and Dyspraxia/DCD - Table 1 Book 6 and www.rcpsych.ac.uk/press/prelease/pr/ pr_238.htm and www.timedoc.net/abstracts/motor_skills.htm

▸▸ Social and communication skills may be affected (see Specific Language Impairment - Book 3); e.g. individuals may:
1. be tactless,
2. appear self-centred (and may not realise how other people view them),
3. appear eccentric to their peer group,
4. talk too much,
5. have difficulties in understanding certain aspects of language such as puns, riddles and jokes,
6. play better with a partner than in a group,
7. have difficulties in understanding 'facial expressions',
8. have difficulties in using the 'tone of voice' as an aid to understanding the emotional state of the talker, When this is combined with not understanding 'facial expressions', they may not realise when someone is becoming angry. Thus, when the person loses their temper it can come as a complete surprise to the individual. They may be unable to tell when somebody is joking with them as they take whatever the person says literally and ignore the tone of voice used. Therefore, they may not always know when someone is being pleasant/unpleasant to them.

Assessment of Attention Deficits

Although there are no set psychological tests for ADHD, there are various criteria used to diagnose it. Professionals commonly use the DSM-IV criteria or their ICD 10 equivalents. Many people are unaware that the means by which the presence of Attention Deficit Hyperactivity Disorder (with or without the presence of Hyperactivity) is diagnosed is through the use of taking a history of the person and then the filling in of a checklist. This diagnosis can be made via various professionals who deal with mental health; e.g. child psychiatrist or via educators who are trained assessors. All of these professionals, especially

Once ADHD students start to 'read' the tone of voice used by people, they may rely upon that as his/her guide to a person's emotional state. Such individuals can find it particularly disturbing if the teacher/parent shouts at another child, because they are always worried that they might be shouted at next. (Also see Specific Language Impairment – Book 3 and Autistic Spectrum Disorder – Chapter 4.)

PART 3 - Referring
A diagnosis can be obtained by the parent asking their GP to refer their child to a community paediatrician, a child psychiatrist, a clinical psychologist or an educational psychologist or other AD/HD specialist. In Scotland the preschool child may be referred to the Child and Family Psychiatry Unit, Yorkhill Hospital, Glasgow. This provides a day-treatment programme for ADHD children and training for Fulton Mackay nurses who specialise in helping such children to modify their antisocial behaviour.

Notes on using ADHD checklists

The assessor can read the checklists to the student/parent if reading difficulties are present. Glaring inconsistencies can be found once the parent and student forms have been completed and this can be quite an 'eye-opener' to all parties. Spending time discussing with the parents and student the differences in answers can:

➤ enable the parents, perhaps for the first time, to see the depth and breadth of the problems that the student is experiencing,

➤ the student can start to perceive the difficulties that the parent is experiencing in trying to cope with his/her behaviours.

Do not presume that the educator's checklist has a greater weighting than that of the parent/student; each checklist is giving the assessor a different perspective on the student and how s/he functions in different environments.

Recommended publications

📖 *Attention Deficit Hyperactivity Disorder* by Dr. P.V.F. Cosgrove (Consultant Child & Adolescent Psychiatrist)

📖 *Understanding Attention Deficit Disorder* by Dr. Christopher Green and Dr Kit Chee (Specialist paediatricians)

📖 *The Hidden Handicap* by Dr Gordon Serfontein (Paediatric neurologist)

📖 *All About ADD – Understanding Attention Deficit Disorder* by Mark Selikowitz (pub. Oxford University Press).

📖 *PRIM: Pre-Referral Intervention Manual* (available from ADDISS - see page 29) contains a wealth of excellent strategies for students with attention deficits.

the educators, must have considerable knowledge of ADHD including knowing enough about associated conditions to recommend referrals to appropriate medical professionals. There are several types of checklist available for this purpose and all require that at least two versions of the checklist (student, parent, educator) are filled in with different student forms being available for different aged students.

This section looks at two of the checklists that are currently available - the **Brown** and the **Conners'**, both of which correlate with the DSM-IV criteria for the different forms of Attention Deficit Disorder (see pages 20-22). They are available from The Psychological Corporation Europe, 32 Jamestown Road, London NW1 7BY (Tel: 020 7424 4456). Both checklists use different sets of sub-tests and so the checklists are actually assessing slightly different things. A very thorough reading of the manuals (which are 'heavy going') is essential before using either of the scales and the assessor should also be very familiar with attention deficit behaviours and the different causes of them. Only certain types of professionals such as psychologists and **Specialist assessor trained educators** (e.g. those holding a OCR or RSA Diploma in SpLD, AMBDA status) can use these checklists. (They have to be registered with The Psychological Corporation). The authoress has found (by using both the Conners' and the Brown on several students) that there is likely to be a high correlation between the two checklists for determining the presence of Attention Deficit Disorder and the relevant sub-groups which are present They both use self carbon marking forms which have to be purchased for each student assessed. The **Brown** requires that an assessment of intelligence is conducted first - with the shortage of educational psychologist appointments that seems to afflict most schools, this might seem to be a problem. However, although only educational psychologists can administer the WISC and the BAS intelligence tests, the specialist assessor trained educators will have had training in assessment including some types of intelligence tests. We also now have some very impressive computer programs that any educator can use which will determine cognitive functioning; (details of which can be found in *Identification Solutions for Literacy* by Jan Poustie, ISBN 1901544036).

Both the **Brown** and the **Conners'** checklists require that the assessor spends time transferring data (and adding up series of totals) on the score sheet - assessors need to allow enough time to do this since it cannot be done in a hurry. Both checklists use T-scores; these allow the assessor to compare the student with students of his/her own age so a T-score of 50 is average for the student's age group and a score of 70 is a well above average likelihood of that difficulty being present. The Psychological Corporation stock a computer program (the *Brown ADD Scales Scoring Assistant*) that generates a brief report and a graph display of the results. The Brown recommends that as part of the assessment process there is a screening for co-morbid psychiatric and learning disorders - the reality is that some assessors actually do not have the experience and expertise (and sometimes the time) to do this - even when they are psychologists or psychiatrists. The *Poustie Identification Checklists* (found in each of the books in the *Identification Solutions for Specific Learning Difficulties Library*) may be used as the first stage of such a screening. The second stage is the reading of comprehensive material, such as this book, so that the assessor is informed as to how these other conditions show themselves and knows to whom s/he must now refer the student. Some of the problems that a raised score in each of the subscales/clusters is likely to indicate are shown below, the higher the score the student achieves the greater the problem will be.

Conners' Rating Scale - Revised (Suitable: 3 – 17 years)
Is a respected, and widely used, tool for the determination of the presence of attention deficits. It is a series of checklists that were first designed in the 1960's with its latest revision being produced in 1997. Each of the checklists looks at a different set of behaviours. The Conners' has a greater variety of checklists than the Brown. The Inattention and Hyperactivity subscales are highly correlated to the DSM-IV criteria. Examples of various subscales are shown below:

Inattention:
More academic difficulties than most individuals of their age and intellectual ability. Difficulties in: organising work, completing tasks, schoolwork, concentrating on tasks that require sustained mental effort.
Hyperactivity:
Difficulties in: sitting still, (may feel more restless and impulsive as compared with most individuals of his/her age and intellectual ability, may frequently have the need to be always 'on the go').
Anxiety/shyness:
Student has more worries and fears than most individuals his/her age. Prone to be emotional, very sensitive to criticism and particularly anxious in new or unfamiliar situations.
Social problems:
According to which items are positive, could indicate low self-esteem, little self-confidence, need for the development and maintenance of friendships to be encouraged and enabled.
Psychosomatic:
Score would be raised if the student is under stress.

Brown Attention-Deficit Disorder Scales (Suitable: 3 - 18 years)
Organising, Prioritising, and Activating to Work
Difficulties in: following directions, organizing and starting academic tasks (e.g. class work), tasks that are not self-selected for fun (e.g. chores in the home).
Focusing, Sustaining, and Shifting Attention to Tasks
Difficulties in: sustaining attention for tasks that are not self-selected, listening comprehension and reading comprehension.
Regulating Alertness, Sustaining Effort, and Processing Speed
Difficulties: sustaining effort, slowness in processing information/sluggishness

Conners' and Brown scales
The time taken to conduct the tests varies but both sets of checklists have short forms and long forms. It is noticeable that encouragement can be needed to keep the ADHD student going when the long forms are used. The **Conners'** uses much simpler sentences than the **Brown** for all its versions. The **Brown** uses simple sentences for the parent and teacher forms but much lengthier, and more complex, sentence structure for the form that is read to the student (adult or child). Therefore, it is best not to use the **Brown** with students who have any of the following difficulties (language impairment, auditory processing difficulties, comprehension difficulties).

when the situation requires sitting still/quietly during academic activities: e.g. writing and reading.

<u>Managing Frustration and Modulating Emotions</u>

Quick to feel annoyance/frustration and express irritation with an intensity that seems excessive for the situation. Vulnerability and sensitivity (e.g. to criticism). Emotions take over brain function so student cannot process information adequately.

<u>Utilising Working Memory and Accessing Recall</u>

Forgetful in daily routines. Difficulties in: keeping several things in memory at once whilst doing a task (e.g. maths word problems, creation of sentences whilst working out the plot of the story), recalling information during exams.

<u>Monitoring and Self-Regulation Action</u>

Difficulties in: pacing action to fit the circumstances for tasks which need more care/slower movements than others; e.g. handwriting and spelling. Unable to 'size up' a situation before acting, unable to recognise the verbal/physical cues from adults that indicate that the student's behaviour is inappropriate.

Help and Support

The Hyperactive Children's Support Group

71 Whyke Lane, Chichester, West Sussex, PO19 2LD
Tel/Fax: 01903 725182. Fax: 01243 552019.
Website: www.hacsg.org.uk
Provides information, support, a newsletter and training.

ADDISS

(National Attention Deficit Disorder Information and Support Service) 10 Station Road, Mill Hill, London NW7 2JU
Tel: 020 8906 9068, Fax: 020 8959 0727
e-mail: info@addiss.co.uk website: www.addiss.co.uk
Stocks a wide range of ADD/ADHD books and holds national conferences.

ADDept

c/o Bob Breen, 30 The Paddock, York YO26 6AW.
Tel: 01904 782 556. Holds an excellent conference every two years for parents and professionals.

The ADHD National Alliance

209 - 211 City Road, London, EC1V 1JN. Tel: 0207 608 8760
e-mail: info@adhdalliance.org.uk website: www.cafamily.org.uk (this is also the website of Contact a Family: a charity that supports families who have children with disabilities and learning difficulties.) The ADHD National Alliance provides information on local groups and issues a regular newsletter. Also see Osteopathy, homeopathy plus Other organisations sections on page 63.

CHADD (Children and Adults with Attention Deficit/ Hyperactivity Disorder)

website: http://www.chadd.org
A well respected US national ADHD support group, provides information, advice and support.

References and Footnotes

1. Unfortunately this pack is no longer available as The AD/HD Family Support Group UK has disbanded.
2. Author's note: or maintains concentration inappropriately; e.g. the person focuses on the task to the exclusion of the needs of those around him. (The person can become so focused that s/ he ignores body signals like hunger until the task is finished.)
3. Author's note: hyperactivity does not always accompany ADHD; e.g. Undifferentiated Attention Deficit Disorder.
4. Dr P.V.F. Cosgrove in *Attention Deficit Hyperactivity Disorder*, the author has added in the words 'adult' and 'adults' as ADHD can carry on into adulthood.
5. Dr P.V.F. Cosgrove in *Attention Deficit Hyperactivity Disorder*.
6. The AD/HD Family Support Group UK.
7. Dr P.V.F. Cosgrove in *Attention Deficit Hyperactivity Disorder*.
8. The AD/HD Family Support Group UK.
9. Dr Christopher Green and Dr Kit Chee: *Understanding Attention Deficit Disorder*.
10. The AD/HD Family Support Group UK.
11. 'Most children with ADHD seem to have a close relative with a similar problem': *Understanding Attention Deficit Disorder* (Dr Christopher Green and Dr Kit Chee).
12. Dr P.V.F. Cosgrove in *Attention Deficit Hyperactivity Disorder*.
13. Author's note: the genetic inheritance factor also means that a child may have one or both parents affected. It can be very hard for ADHD parents to cope with their own emotions whilst trying to cope with those of their child. Meanwhile their partner can find both spouse and child exhausting!
14. Dr P.V.F. Cosgrove in *Attention Deficit Hyperactivity Disorder*.
15. Dr Christopher Green, Exeter lecture, UK lecture tour 1996.
16. Author's note: getting these children to sleep can be an art in itself and by the time it has been achieved with a hyperactive ADHD baby the parent can be so exhausted that it takes all of the forty-five minutes of the baby's afternoon nap to recover from the exertion. Such babies do not happily lie in their cots and look at the mobiles!
17. Dr P.V.F. Cosgrove in *Attention Deficit Hyperactivity Disorder*.
18, 19 & 20. The AD/HD Family Support Group UK.
21. Dr Christopher Green, Exeter lecture, UK lecture tour 1996.
22. The AD/HD Family Support Group UK.
23. The AD/HD Family Support Group UK.
24. *Understanding Attention Deficit Disorder*, by Drs Green and Chee has a great deal of information on medication.
25. Author's note: see page 58 for the address of The Society of Homeopaths if you wish to go along this route.
26. The author does provide coaching for AD/HD students.
27. Author's note: the idea that their child (or they themselves as an adult) have a psychiatric disorder can be particularly threatening in the UK where psychiatrists are seen by some to be a threat and an American fad rather than highly trained and helpful professionals. As a society we will need to come to terms with the psychiatric side of ADHD if we are to achieve full recognition and treatment of this disorder.
28. The AD/HD Family Support Group UK.
29. Dr P.V.F. Cosgrove in *Attention Deficit Hyperactivity Disorder*.

CHAPTER 4
Autistic Spectrum Disorder

Various terms are used to describe this condition. In the past the term Autistic Continuum Disorder was favoured, which was then replaced by Autistic Spectrum Disorder. The spectrum is wide with only a few people meeting the criteria for classical Autism. The two main providers of diagnostic criteria refer to this condition as Pervasive Developmental Disorder. A sub-group of it is Pervasive Developmental Disorder Not Otherwise Specified (PDD.NOS) which is used when some of the criteria for PDD are not met.

PART 1 – Understanding

Autistic Spectrum Disorder (ASD) is a complex condition that occurs in all classes, creeds and races. It is generally believed to affect four times as many boys as girls (though some evidence shows that the number of girls affected is greater than this). [1] It consists of a broad spectrum of communication disorders that has many components, which are sometimes referred to as subgroups. [2] Although there appears to be an element of overlapping between these subgroups, each of them has unique characteristics and separate names, for example, Asperger's Syndrome and autism. [3]

The condition as a whole represents a pattern of abnormal development typified by difficulties (impairments) in the three areas of social interaction, social communication and imagination. These difficulties occur in varying degrees, ranging from low-level to severe. This 'triad of impairments' unfolds over time (usually appearing in the first two to three years of life) with there often being indications of developmental problems in the first year (see Table 1).

Incidence of Autistic Spectrum Disorder
The incidence of individuals who come within the Autistic Spectrum is rapidly increasing and no-one is sure why this is happening. Just how many are affected is a figure that no-one seems to know. If we compare figures for the past seven years compiled by researchers [4] with those compiled from UK health authority data [5] it is only too apparent that we have a major problem. Even within this data there are big variations; e.g. one health authority had a rate of 1 in 69 for boys aged three years whilst others reported an incidence of one in every 250 children (boys and girls combined). What is obvious from the figures is that several authorities were reporting a bulge in the pre-school group. But why the increase? This question has been puzzling everyone and, just as in ADHD, elements within the environment such as food, chemicals and metals seem to be relevant here (see pages 31-32 for details).

There is no one uniformly accepted belief as to the cause of ASD. In the past, ASD was thought to have been a totally psychological illness but it is now only too apparent that the condition has varying causal factors. Some believe that brain dysfunction of some kind is involved and/or that there is an over-production of a certain chemical in the brain that blocks the normal transmissions within it. There is now an increasing belief that a main cause of ASD is related to chemical and dietary factors. It is not always easy to recognise Autistic Spectrum Disorder because other conditions can mask it and its presentation changes over time.

the large increase in autism and attention deficit disorder during the last decade of the twentieth century. (Also see http://home.earthlink.net/~berniew1/addsum.html) There is also concern now about whether the brain of the developing foetus is being affected by mercury in the diet of the mother. Here the concern is that our polluted waters are causing an increase in the amount of mercury found in large oily fish. This is especially the case with the large types of fish which live longer and contain a lot of oil in their flesh (and so accumulate more mercury in their flesh); e.g. tuna and swordfish. The concern is that the mercury found in fish (methylmercury) is accumulated more easily in the human body than other types of mercury. (See Daily Telegraph 19th February 2004 for further details). It certainly looks as though, in the future, the area of environmental factors (and their contribution to the increasing incidence of autism) is going to be an important aspect of the research into this condition.

Problems common to both Attention Deficit and Autistic Spectrum Disorder students are difficulties in:

▸▸   seeing the other person's point of view;

▸▸   understanding body language;

▸▸   working as part of a team.

Are there any medical conditions which are associated with Autistic Spectrum Disorder?

Yes, therefore it is essential that an individual is referred to a paediatrician if Autistic Spectrum Disorder is suspected as s/he can then exclude any other underlying medical disorder/s that may be associated with Autistic Spectrum Disorder; for example, Fragile-X Syndrome (see Book 1), tuberous sclerosis (see page 39), neurofibromatosis (see Book 6), German Measles (congenital rubella), PKU (see www.pkunews.org/), epilepsy (see http://www.e-epilepsy.org.uk) and Hypomelanosis of Ito (see www.emedicine.com/derm/topic186.htm

What learning difficulties are associated with Autistic Spectrum Disorder?

There appears to be a strong relationship between severe/profound learning difficulties and Autistic Spectrum Disorder. About half of those with such learning difficulties have both conditions. However, of those individuals who have mild learning difficulties, less than one per cent of them will also have Autistic Spectrum Disorder. [8] Individuals who have Autistic Spectrum Disorder can also have various other conditions that affect learning; for example:

▸▸   Hyperlexia (where the individual can read much better than s/he can understand written text); [9]

▸▸   Specific Language Impairment (see Book 3);

▸▸   Dyslexia (see Book 4);

▸▸   Dyspraxia/DCD (see Book 6);

▸▸   Attention Deficit Disorder (see Chapters 2 and 3).

▸▸   Tourette Syndrome (see Chapter 1).

Dentistry work may need to be conducted under general anaesthetic.

About ten per cent of individuals have a special skill far above any of their other abilities; e.g. in music, art, numerical calculations, jigsaw puzzles, [12] dates and such like. A few will be 'savants' – individuals of exceptionally high skill in one narrow area. Interests usually involve classifying information. Hobbies may include activities such as train-spotting, stamp-collecting and the dates of all Manchester United football matches.

Having an advocate can enable higher-functioning individuals (including those with Asperger's Syndrome) to live an independent life. Advocates provide a range of help; e.g. they might go with the individual to important meetings such as seeing the bank manager etc. Local groups of The National Autistic Society can advise on local advocacy services. (See pages 38 and 58 for further details.)

How is Autistic Spectrum Disorder related to intellectual ability?

Autism is present across the intellectual levels. Thus individuals can range 'from being severely learning disabled to being of normal or even superior intelligence'. [10] Various skills are associated with Autistic Spectrum Disorder; for example, individuals may have dexterity in manipulating objects and good visuo-spatial or rote memory skills. [11]

What happens when the child becomes an adult?

For some of those affected by Autistic Spectrum Disorder there will be opportunities to attend college and university (see www.users.dircon.co.uk/~cns/ which is a website for university students with Autism and Asperger's Syndrome).

The future for this group of individuals is very varied. Some of the higher functioning adults who have Asperger's Syndrome may work (some in demanding jobs). They will need a supportive work environment and will need to use advocacy services (see page 63) as they move towards an independent life. Some, of those with classical autism such as those termed 'savants', may reach a high level of expertise in a narrow area of interest. However, the majority do not usually develop the level of social and communication skills necessary to hold down a job equal to their knowledge base.

Autistic Spectrum Disorder 'creates a lifelong need' for the individuals and their families. The majority of individuals will need to live and work in environments where special provision is made for them. However, the availability of such long-term provision is so scarce that it is the parents who may have to meet the bulk of such provision at present and this can become a considerable problem once the parents start to age. It is essential that individuals are introduced to using advocacy services in their teens/early adulthood so that they have advocates available to them when they need them (see page 63). It is important that all those who work with adults who have Autistic Spectrum Disorder are aware that they can become isolated, distressed and depressed in adulthood if adequate provision is not made. (See page 10 for information on depression.)

All working with these students need to be aware that lack of diagnosis and intervention puts individuals (and their families and educators) under immense strain as they struggle to cope with low self-esteem, difficulties with adjusting to change, and problems in relating and communicating with those around them.

Help and Support for Autistic Spectrum Disorder (including Asperger's Syndrome) See pages 43.

Identification Solutions for Behaviour by Jan Poustie   ISBN 1 901544 82 6

PART 2 – Identifying

Is recognition easy?

No, because Autistic Spectrum Disorder neither affects the appearance of the person nor does it present in the same way throughout the individual's life. Furthermore, other conditions that can be found alongside it, such as Dyspraxia/DCD, can mask the signs. Individuals usually look alert, attractive and intelligent,[13] and high intelligence similarly can mask the signs and make it much more difficult to recognise. Although the symptoms usually appear before they are three years old, the changing nature of autism, with different aspects being more obvious at some ages than at others, may make it difficult to make a firm diagnosis. [14] This change in the dominant features may also result with the diagnosis being changed from one component of Autistic Spectrum Disorder to that of another as the individual develops.

Apart from the obvious severe cases it requires a great deal of knowledge to recognise the signs in those children/adults with moderate to low-level difficulties. Also, high intelligence can mask the signs and make it much more difficult to recognise. A stumbling block to recognition and diagnosis can be the failure of everyone to see the 'whole' picture that the child is presenting. The parents may not know what information is important to the professional and during consultation the child may not exhibit the behaviour that can enable an accurate diagnosis to be made. Diagnosis is also made difficult by the similarities of Autistic Spectrum Disorder to certain other conditions; for example:

�» **Specific Language Impairment,** in which language is delayed but social development is relatively normal (see Book 3);

�» **Learning disability/difficulties,** in which all skills are delayed.

The characteristics found in some individuals may only fit part of the pattern of autism, and in such cases the individual may not fulfil the total criteria to diagnose classical autism itself; e.g.

1. **Atypical autism** (*also known as other pervasive developmental disorder*): development is abnormal in all three key areas, with the picture not quite being that of classical autism. Only one or two autistic features are present and onset usually occurs after three years of age.

2. **Asperger's Syndrome**: intelligence and early language development are fairly normal, or above average. Individuals try to be sociable and clumsiness is present (see Chapter 6).

3. **Autistic Features** (Autistic tendencies): the individual

Although difficulties in social integration and the use of language are usually found 'there is no single feature, that if not present, excludes autism.' [15] Occasionally, the individual can show behaviour that we would expect to see in non-autistic individuals, such as making eye contact, using perfect grammar, cuddling someone (see page 41). It is the usual, 'overall pattern of the individual that is relevant'. [16] Odd intonation is likely, as are difficulties in understanding systems of non-verbal communication, e.g. gestures. [17] (Also see Fragile-X Syndrome – Book 1.)

Identification Solutions for Behaviour by Jan Poustie   ISBN 1 901544 82 6

Inappropriate interaction with others is a key indicator. A wide range of behaviours can be seen; e.g. complete withdrawal, passivity (the child will allow others to 'play with him/her' in roles that require no interaction; e.g. being a baby), repeated pestering, rejection or fear of other people, making inappropriate social approaches. This latter group show various behaviours; e.g. they may talk at people (usually those in authority rather than their peers) and may have difficulties in making and/or breaking eye contact appropriately. In adolescence and adulthood, those individuals who are the most able (and who have good language skills) may become overformal in their social interactions; e.g., be over-polite even to family members. [24]

falls into the grey area where a firm diagnosis either way cannot be made. [18]

4. **Childhood Disintegrative Disorder**: development is normal up to two years, but then there is a loss of two or more of certain skills such as play, social skills, language, motor skills and bowel/bladder control. [19]

Assessment of intellectual functioning can aid diagnosis. The higher intellectual functioning individual with autism is likely to have a markedly higher non-verbal functioning as compared with his verbal ability. The individual with Asperger's Syndrome is likely to have average (or above average) intelligence and tends to have a similar level of non-verbal and verbal functioning. [20] Wing suggests that, from the individual's point of view, it is not particularly relevant to closely define the subgroup to which an individual belongs. Instead, the aim of an assessment should be to decide if Autistic Spectrum Disorder is present and then to concentrate on assessing his/her abilities [21] for such an assessment helps decide appropriate provision.

Indicators of Autistic Spectrum Disorder

➤ Some individuals never speak and for the rest delayed speech development is common. [22] Unusual language/speech patterns associated with Specific Language Impairment may be seen, especially Semantic Pragmatic Disorder. For example, individuals may be very literal in their own speech and in their understanding of other people's speech and of written information; they may exhibit delayed speech; meaninglessly echo phrases that have been said by others (echolalia); use the wrong personal pronouns; and talk 'at' or 'question' people rather than converse with them.

➤ There is debate as to whether Semantic-Pragmatic Disorder can exist without Autistic Spectrum Disorder being present. [23] (See *Pragmatic Language Impairment Without Autism: the Children in Question* by Nicola Botting and Gina Conti-Ramsden, University of Manchester, UK at http://www.sagepub.co.uk/journals/Details/issue/sample/a010438.pdf and http://www.hcd.man.ac.uk/langlab/transitions.htm

Some students may be diagnosed as having Higher-Level Language Disorder (HLLD), in the past this was sometimes called Higher Level Language Impairment (HLL)) see Book 3 and www.afasic.org.uk

➤ Some individuals exhibit difficulties in putting themselves in 'someone else's shoes' - being able to see the other person's viewpoint.

▸ Some individuals exhibit difficulties in relating to other people.

▸ Some individuals may be inflexible - exhibiting a dislike of any change in routine, and insisting on certain routines occurring, such as following an identical route to certain places, a lengthy bedtime ritual or the repetition of a sequence of odd bodily movements. [25]

▸ Some individuals may exhibit an unusually intense interest in a narrow area of a topic, for example, dimensions of castles

▸ Some individuals may exhibit difficulties in any tasks that require the use of the imagination.

▸ Some individuals may exhibit difficulties in using 'abstract' thoughts and symbolic language.

▸ Some individuals may be more interested in objects than people, especially when they are young.

▸ Some individuals may exhibit difficulties in judging the motivations, intentions and sensitivities of others.

The child may be delayed in (or never show) pointing behaviour. (Normally, at about 12–18 months, children use pointing as a way of drawing the carer's attention to an object or an event in which s/he is interested.) If 'pointing' is delayed, or does not occur (and this behaviour is limited to the child's own interests) then Autistic Spectrum Disorder should be suspected. [28] The child may hand-lead. This can be used instead of pointing. The child takes the hand of the carer (but does not look at them): then takes the hand to an object of interest; for example, a bag that s/he wants opened.

The child
The baby's behaviour can range widely. A very small number are irritable and difficult to soothe, most are quiet and exceptionally good and there are a few who fit neither group. The 'full picture' is not likely to emerge until s/he starts to walk independently, as until then the range of a child's behaviour is limited. [26] As s/he gets older, s/he may seem detached and aloof and appear to see people as 'objects to be used' rather than as people with their own set of needs and emotions.

Common indicators in children (some of which will carry on past this developmental stage)

Babies and toddlers may show any of the following: [27]

▸ dislike being interfered with (for example, nappy changing, bathing, dressing etc.);

▸ smile at something but not smile when looking at a person's face;

▸ be fascinated by (and/or show inappropriate distress) to visual and auditory stimuli, such as lights, television, music.
Inappropriate response to auditory stimuli can also be seen alongside Dyslexia (Book 4), Auditory Processing Disorder (Book 3), Attention Deficit Disorder (Chapters 1 and 2) and Dyspraxia/DCD (Book 6);

▸ have feeding problems. Signs of Oral/Verbal(Articulatory) Dyspraxia may be present, such as sucking, chewing and swallowing difficulties (see Books 3 and 6). Children with a

The ASD child may not smile, or may smile at inappropriate times.

ASD children may like being cuddled (but *only* when they want it). They do not use this as a form of social interaction and seem unaware of the feelings of others. They do not look at the parent whilst being cuddled (non-Autistic Spectrum Disorder children will indicate that they are happy through sounds/words and through looking at the parent's face)

combination of severe visual and hearing impairment can also reject lumpy food [29] (see Books 4 and 6). [30]

▸▸ after being frustrated or punished, they may suddenly stop crying without the parent intervening to calm him/her;

▸▸ exhibit delayed social behaviour (or this may not exist at all). 'Play' will be affected; for example, they may ignore other children, or play 'alongside' them long after these forms of play are normally replaced by others types by (e.g. after the age of four years). They will have to be taught how to play with toys. They may not show imaginative/creative play behaviour (or such play will be very limited). In pretend play, they will not pretend to paint with an object that is being used as a paintbrush. They may like physical play; for example, being tickled, chasing, jumping etc.

▸▸ not imitate other people's behaviour, so at twelve months they are unlikely to have learnt to wave 'bye-bye'. They are unlikely to learn practical skills by being told and/or shown how to do them (difficulties in learning practical skills are also common in Dyspraxia/DCD – see Book 6) but they can learn if they are physically guided by the carer.

The school child may show any of the following signs:

▸▸ be very independent at a young age; too independent for the parent's peace of mind. Most young children like to stay close to their parents, especially in unfamiliar situations, but the child with Autistic Spectrum Disorder may venture too far away from them. (This can also occur as part of Attention Deficit Disorder see Chapters 2 and 3);

▸▸ actively avoid the parent's company;

▸▸ not seek comfort from parents in stressful situations;

▸▸ constantly asking questions, sometimes asking the same series of questions and demanding the same standard answers regarding topics that fascinate them. (Pre-school non-autistic children aged between 3–5 years also ask many questions, but they do not become upset if the answer to the question differs slightly);

▸▸ have irrational fears of particular objects and/or situations which may continue for a long time. (This is different from the fears that very young non-Autistic Spectrum children can have, where the fear is related to something obvious that is frightening them; for example, being frightened of a lamp because its shadow distorted on the wall. Once the explanation has been given and the lamp moved, so that the distorted shadow no longer appears, the fear of the non-ASD child goes away);

▸▸ have an unusual 'learning curve'. Normally, progress can be plotted on a graph as a curve, which may have one or two straight horizontal lines (called plateaus) that mark a certain length of time when no progress occurred. In ASD children there are far more plateaus than usual and each lasts for a long time. Skills can also suddenly appear without any practice of the task; [31]

▸▸ have difficulties in knowing the passage of time; for example, s/he cannot 'wait' for something, is unable to complete a task within a given amount of time, or is unable to cope with the idea of the future and that all things have a beginning and, more importantly, an end. Such individuals rely heavily on a timetable and cannot cope when circumstances mean that the timetable has to be changed in any way;

▸▸ able to realise where they (and their possessions) are in the dark and may be able to walk/cycle etc. without appearing to look where they are going;

▸▸ ASD children may only eat a few foods and may only try out new foods if they are a particular colour. They may refuse to eat their favourite food if it is prepared differently. (Also see metabolic dysfunctioning and food intolerances – Book 1.)

▸▸ appear aloof. They may ignore people unless they want the person to do something for them. They also may ignore people's reactions to events and so cannot respond appropriately to happiness or sadness in others. [32] They may also ignore other people's reactions to their own behaviour (so do not come when called or react when told off). A child may have his/her behaviour incorrectly interpreted as disobedience by adults; in other words, the child can exhibit emotional indifference/aloofness, doing what s/he wants to do when s/he wants to do it.;

▸▸ make eye contact but will not use facial expressions and 'gaze' as part of his/her system of non-verbal communication;

▸▸ not take part in social interactions with others by smiling or making sounds;

▸▸ not try to provoke an emotional reaction from others, or show how s/he feels (s/he may not point at things, vocalise at interesting items or take them to show his/her carer);

▸▸ be uninterested in others praising his/her successes;

▸▸ be unable to tell the difference between positive and negative emotions;

▸▸ have a great need for reassurance but not understand/respond to common forms of showing this; e.g. explanations, cuddles etc.

▸▸ repeatedly replay the same parts of a video or CD, and repetitively act out characters from popular television series; [33]

▸▸ have good and bad days, in common with most of the other conditions that come within the SpLD Profile.

Books that use cartoons/picture strips to help the student understand social skills and such like are:

📖 *Teaching Children with Autism to Mind-read – a Practical Guide* by Patricia Howlin, Simon Baron-Cohen and Julie Hadwin (ISBN 0 471 97623 7, pub. by John Wiley & Sons Ltd., Chichester, UK).

📖 *The New Social Story Book* – by Carol Gray (ISBN 119-3495-98, pub. by Winslow . Press). Contains stories written to explain the social aspects of situations and incorporates instructions on how to help the person deal with a problem they have in a specific area.

📖 *Comic Strip Conversations* by Carol Gray, (ISBN 119-3495-98, pub: Winslow Press). Uses stick-men illustrations to help children to express their thoughts/ feelings and explains how conversations and interruptions work.

For other books on Autistic Spectrum Disorder see page 44.

Case study: Tina

(Tina is a young adult who has both Autism and Tuberous Sclerosis.)

Individuals may perform rituals with the body of their carer.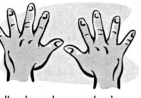

Tina repeatedly places her mother's hands in a particular position on her lap. Every time the mother tries to move, Tina gazes at her face and then places her mother's hands back on to her lap. For over six years the authoress has seen Tina at irregular intervals but it is only in the last few months that Tina has started to use the above behaviour with the authoress. (Different rituals occur according to the location. Thus there is one particular house will Tina will insist on a serviette being placed on her lap before eating and drinking.)

Tuberous Sclerosis (TS)

This is also referred to as tuberous sclerosis complex (TSC) to distinguish tuberous sclerosis from Tourette Syndrome. For information on TSC go to: http://www.tsalliance.org/faq.asp

Any, or all, of the following may also be seen at various stages in development:

▸   inappropriate reactions to stimuli; for example, laughing at the wrong things *(this can also be a sign of embarrassment)*, unreasonable fears and becoming upset, also becoming overly fascinated by various objects; for example, spinning objects, particular forms of light and movement (such as tree branches, the effect of light and shade as a car passes under a series of motorway bridges) and their own hands.

▸   do not lie or say uncomplicated or non-manipulative lies,

▸   unusual movements. Many young children will demonstrate occasional unusual movements as part of a phase of development; when that phase finishes so do the movements. However, the individual with ASD will continue with such movements as: walking stiffly, walking on tiptoe, twirling his/her body around, rocking, head-banging or flapping parts of his/her body, especially when feeling strong emotions such as excitement or when fascinated by something.

'Hand-flapping', 'finger-flapping' and 'arm-flapping' are very distinctive movements that, once seen, are never forgotten, as they look so unusual. Some individuals flap their hands or fingers; others may flap their arms (some do all of these.)

Finger-flapping is a flicking of the fingers that imitates the movement of rain falling. Hand-flapping is the whole hand being flapped from the wrist with the fingers being kept loose. When hand-/finger-flapping occurs, the arms may be held rigid, with the elbows bent tightly upward (it looks a bit like a chicken flapping its wings) or the arms may be extended and the elbows locked. Arm-flapping is a flapping of the whole arm (upper or lower part or both parts together).

▸   looking at an object at very close range as though it cannot be seen it properly (but can spot sweets with ease!).

▸   making collections of objects (such as pebbles) and arranging them in lines or patterns.

▸   seeming to be unaware of certain sounds, but being immediately aware of certain sounds/words, such as the word 'chocolate'!

▸   using objects inappropriately (for example, stroking, sniffing, licking or kissing a spade instead of digging with it; becoming attached to odd objects rather than a cuddly toy).

▸   having a lack of fear about realistic dangers.

▸   using gestures to 'ask' for something rather than using speech.

▸   appearing rude, boring or pompous when talking to others.

▸ seeking isolation when distressed and frightened rather than seeking comfort from their carers.

▸ expecting routine in those around him/her; for example, expecting them always to sit in the same seats in the car.

▸ showing an inappropriate response to sensory stimuli; for example, the individual may be indifferent/oversensitive to pain, temperature and hunger pangs. (See Dyspraxia/DCD - Book 6 and Attention Deficit Disorder - Chapters 2 and 3.) The individual may also be indifferent to sound or 'hyperacusis' (an oversensitivity to sound) may be present. (see Auditory Processing Disorder - Book 3.)

▸ a dislike of being looked at by others.

▸ self-injurious behaviours can be shown by a few individuals; for example, head-banging, hand-biting, hitting one side of the head and repetitive scratching. (However, it should be remembered that occasional examples of the first three can also be seen as the result of severe frustration and that scratching can also be an indicator of an allergic reaction/ eczema.)

▸ behaviour that is worse in unstructured environments (thus, it may well be worse at home than in the school or the clinic). [34]

▸ excessive drinking of liquids – this may lead to vomiting.

Indicators which may be seen but which could also indicate Attention Deficit Disorder - (see Chapters 2 and 3)

▸ severe temper tantrums (can also be the result of severe frustration).

▸ marked food fads (with often only very few foods being accepted) that are very difficult to change and persist for a long time. (Normally food fads start at about two years of age and disappear by the age of five or six years.)

▸ refusal to obey instructions (also see Oppositional Defiant Disorder - page 70).

▸ defiant and/or aggressive behaviour; for example, running away, screaming, biting or kicking other people. (Also see Oppositional Defiant Disorder - page 70.) They can also destroy and/or interfere with other people's possessions.

▸ sleeping difficulties; for example, an inability to get to sleep with ease, waking up frequently during the night, a dislike of going to bed.

▸ constantly interrupting others.

▸ difficulties in maintaining attention appropriately; possibly also an ability to focus attention on particular tasks for an unusually long length of time.

▸ anxiety.

Both Attention Deficit and Autistic Spectrum Disorder students can lack fear and not recognise danger. This can be extremely wearing on their carers.

ASD individuals may become more isolated and obsessional as they get older.

Identification Solutions for Behaviour by Jan Poustie   ISBN 1 901544 82 6

No matter which condition is present, recognition (followed by diagnosis), is the first step along a road which should enable everyone involved to have easier, and greater, access to information help and support. The individual will still place great demands upon parenting skills, the family and the student's educators but now they will be in a position to access local support groups and families. Upon diagnosis appropriate provision (including respite care if necessary) should be able to be obtained but this does not always occur, see Case Study Kevin, page 42.

‣ difficulties in using gestures and body language, and in understanding their use by others.

‣ poor memory skills.

Indicators that may also indicate Dyslexia - see Book 4.

‣ anxiety (this is also associated with highly intelligent female Dyslexics in the 8-12-year-old group – see Book 3).

‣ poor memory skills.

‣ difficulties in sequencing.

Indicators that may also indicate Dyspraxia/DCD - see Book 6.

‣ The various forms of Dyspraxia/DCD can be present, with both fine-motor and/or gross-motor control difficulties being seen. There can be a noticeable difficulty with the playing of team games where coordination of one's own actions with those of others, plus an understanding of the rules of the game, is necessary. [35] It would seem likely that part of this problem is a difficulty in spatial relationships (for example, Constructional Dyspraxia, see Book 6) and Receptive Language Difficulties/Auditory Processing Disorder – see Book 3.)

‣ over/under reaction to any or all of the following: touch, taste, smell and temperature.

‣ little attention paid to appearance (Dressing Dyspraxia may be present) or a failure to put the final touches to appearance (also see Book 6).

‣ difficulties in turn-taking in games and in understanding the rules of games.

‣ being a loner.

‣ failing to understand 'social distance' – getting too close or too far away from people.

‣ motor coordination difficulties (clumsiness is commonly associated with Asperger's Syndrome, see Chapter 6).

‣ Meaninglessly copying other people's movements (echopraxia).

Case study: Lisa

Assessment is the first positive step along the road to change and future success. Lisa's mother had held concerns about her preschool child for some time. She had mentioned her worries to her GP and her Health Visitor, but both felt that there was no cause for concern. One of the staff of the Montisorri Nursery School, which Lisa attended, suggested that the mother read the first edition of this book. Once the mother had read the chapter on Autistic Spectrum Disorder she had the confidence to demand an assessment for Lisa via her GP. As a result of this referral, Lisa, at age three years, was diagnosed as having Autism.

Case study: Kevin

Kevin has Asperger's Syndrome. He was very unhappy at his primary school; his mother felt this was as a result of his condition not being appropriately provided for. She took him out of school and home educated him. When she asked the social worker for respite care she was told that she would not be able to have any until her son started attending school again. An appropriate solution in this case, which would have taken a lot of the pressure off of the mother, would have been for the Local Education Authority to provide home tuition and the social worker to provide the respite care. It is a sad state of affairs that some schools and social work departments do not provide adequately when ASD is present, staff training is needed here if we are ever to see such situations turn around.

PART 3 – Referring

It is important that the assessment is seen as the first positive step along the road to change and future success. Parents need to be made aware that through appropriate intervention their child will continue to change and grow and develop new abilities. Cultural factors will affect the parent's reaction to diagnosis and may cause parents from some ethnic groups to find it very difficult to come to terms with it. [36]

How is Autistic Spectrum Disorder diagnosed?

Diagnostic questionnaires and checklists are used to determine the presence of ASD (see www.health.state.ny.us/nysdoh/eip/autism/screenin.htm and page 44 reference 37).

ASD is an evolving diagnosis and so those with the condition may see a series of professionals over a number of years. Since delayed language development is commonly associated with ASD, it is likely that the first professional to assess the student will be a Speech and Language Therapist. (Thus, professionals need to be on the look-out for ASD if a diagnosis has already been made of Semantic-Pragmatic Disorder or Higher-Level Language Impairment.) Some students are recognised very early on, as Lisa's case study showed. Once the ASD indicators have been spotted, it is essential that the child is referred for specialist diagnosis and assessment as early as possible.

There may be a need for two referrals:

▸ A referral to diagnose the presence of ASD can be achieved through the local GP referring the child to a local paediatrician who has an interest in this field. The local paediatrician will then arrange for the child to have a multidisciplinary assessment, which will include representation from the local education authority. The referral process can also be started by a teacher contacting the school doctor.

A 'framework' is vital for these individuals.

We can enable the Autistic Spectrum individual to reach his/her potential by changing the task and the environment to meet his/her needs. Diagnosis enables the introduction of a 'framework' that promotes structure, routine and continuity, and the possibility of very gradual changes being introduced. This 'framework' enables individuals to understand and communicate with the world around them and thus reduces their levels of anxiety. It provides bridging mechanisms by which they can cross from their own unique environment into that of others and so helps the individual to reach his/her potential, as well as improving the quality of life for all.

Teaching/communication methods

Approximately one in twenty-four children will be severe enough to attend a special unit/school for part of their education. Most students will attend a school for children with moderate/severe learning difficulties. The more able child, and the child with few management problems, is likely to attend mainstream primary and/or secondary school, but his/her social difficulties can make him/her more vulnerable, so appropriate support will be necessary. Various teaching methods can be used; e.g. TEACCH (see www.teacch.com/ and www.autismuk.com). A useful communication strategy is the PECS system, see www.pecs-uk.com

Help and Support for Autistic spectrum disorder (including Asperger's syndrome)

The National Autistic Society
393 City Road, London EC1V 1NG.
Tel: 020 7833 2299; Fax: 0207 833 9666; Helpline: 0870 6008585; Information Service (for professionals working with children and adults): 0207 9033599; Websites: General information: www.nas.org.uk Provides conferences, in-service training and support. There is a huge amount of information on the website on both the condition and how to manage it, including very useful sections for educators. Website for professional researchers: ww.autismconnect.org
Scottish Society for Autistic Children
Hilton House, Alloa Business Park, Whins Road, Alloa, FK10 3SA.

➤ If it is thought that the student belongs to the second category of ASD; that is, those students who have food intolerances and such like; then a referral will have to be made to specialists who deal with this aspect of autism.

At present there are few specialists in either of these fields and the second type of referral may have to be to private specialists which can be costly. Professionals and parents can gain help and support from the various charities that deal with ASD and language difficulties; for example, The National Autistic Society (see left-hand column) and Afasic (see page 63).

A diagnosis depends upon obtaining a detailed history of the child's development, a careful assessment of skills and abilities [37] and consideration of all the different aspects of the child's behaviour in a systematic way. This is likely to include a lengthy interview with the parents (about two to three hours), observation of the individual's behaviour and psychological testing. It is important that such an assessment is not rushed; if it is, the evidence of autism may be missed. [38] Ideally, a multidisciplinary assessment is conducted to assess the child throughout his/her preschool/school years. This can involve many people, such as paediatric neurologist, child psychiatrist, psychologist, speech and language/physio/occupational therapists, social worker, teacher and parents. [39]

What happens next?

An effective working partnership of parents and professionals (with the parents being **actively involved** as much as possible) will be needed to provide the step-by-step intervention that will enable the individual's difficulties to be addressed. At present there is considerable variation between the provision being offered by the various Local Education Authorities (LEA's). Ideally, input is needed from the following sectors:

Health services: Clinical support for the problems will be needed. Intervention of a clinical psychologist and a psychiatrist, each of whom is experienced in this field, should occur. Medication may be recommended if behavioural difficulties such as aggression and temper tantrums are severe/prolonged/frequent and cannot be reduced by removing the cause of them.

Social services: A service plan should be created to ensure that the child's needs are met. This will include intensive and individual therapeutic programmes that involve parents and professionals, effective family support and respite care. The same sort of plan is needed for the families of students who have severe (or several) forms of the conditions found in this book.

Education: Specialised teaching approaches are vital; [40] a Statement of Special Educational Needs may be necessary (see Book 2).

Recommended reading/video

📖 *Autism: The Facts* by Dr Simon Baron-Cohen and Dr Patrick Bolton (pub. by Oxford University Press).

📖 *Could This Be Autism?* (booklet) and *Autism: How to help your young child* - both pub. The National Autistic Society

📖 *Autistic Spectrum Disorders: an Aid to Diagnosis* by Lorna Wing (pub. by The National Autistic Society).

📖 *The Autistic Spectrum: a guide for Parents and Professionals* by Lorna Wing (pub. by Constable Publishers).

📖 *The World of the Autistic Child* by Bryna Siegel (pub. by Oxford University Press).

📖 *Solving Behaviour Problems in Autism - Improving Communication with Visual Strategies* by Linda A Hodgdon. (ISBN 0 9616786 2 3, pub. by Quirk Roberts Publishing. (In the UK from Winslow Press Tel: 01869 244644).

📖 *Dear Psychiatrist..... Do child care specialists understand?* Jennie Roberts The Lutterworth Press ISBN 0-7188-2935-2 - Written in the form of a letter from a mother to her son's psychiatrist; highlights problems faced by parents of a child with special needs, misunderstanding by professionals; the battle many families face in getting the right kind of help/support for a child whose difficulties are not obvious.

📖 *I am Special - Introducing children and young people to their Autistic Spectrum Disorder* - Peter Vermeulen ISBN 1-85302-916-5 (Jessica Kingsley Publishers). For use by professionals for children aged 12+ years.

📖 *The Autism File* published by Sensinet Ltd. (e-mail: info@autismfile.com. Tel: 01208 979 2525)

📖 *Children with autism: 2nd Ed.* - Trevarthen, Aitken et.al. :Jessica Kingsley Publishers. Practical guide for teaching.

📖 *Children with autism and Asperger's Syndrome* : A guide for practitioners and carers. - P. Howlin: John Wiley & Sons ISBN 0-471983-28-4 Lots of information but quite a heavy read.

📖 *Teaching children with autism: Strategies to enhance communicaton and socialization* by K A Quill

📹 *Autism: a World Apart* (Channel 4) a useful video to watch.

References & Footnotes:

1. There is a possibility that the ratio is more like two boys for every girl (with girls being more difficult to recognise than boys). For further information see "*The Autistic Spectrum: a guide for professionals and parents*" by Lorna Wing (pub. Constable).

2. The term Autistic Spectrum Disorder is used in the UK/Europe, in the USA the term Pervasive Developmental Disorders is used.

3. Although it is agreed by many professionals that all these conditions share similarities it is argued that the assumption that they all represent some variant of autism is unproved and may not be useful. The reply to this argument is that research by psychologists increasingly points to a complex, broad but specific cognitive ability called 'concept of mind' underpinning all autistic-like conditions. (AFASIC Glossary sheets 8 & 16)

4. See *Autism - a world apart* (video produced by Poseidon Film Productions, Distributed by Hopeline Videos), the statistics at http://osiris.sunderland.ac.uk/autism/incidence.htm and "*The Autistic Spectrum: a guide for professionals and parents*" by Lorna Wing (pub. Constable).

5. For further information http://www.autismuk.com/index30.htm

6. & 7. *Could this be Autism* (pub. by The National Autistic Society).

8. See "*The Autistic Spectrum: a guide for professionals and parents*" by L Wing.

9. *Could this be Autism* (pub. by The National Autistic Society).

10. Naomi Richman- *Autism: making an early diagnosis* (pub. in The Practitioner 23/05/1988, Vol. 232)

11. See "*The Autistic Spectrum: a guide for professionals and parents*" by L Wing.

12. *Could this be Autism* (pub. by The National Autistic Society)

13. These features are included in Kanner's original description of autism. For further information see page 19 *The Autistic Spectrum: a guide for professionals and parents* by Lorna Wing (pub. Constable).

14. e.g. impairment of social relationships being most noticeable before the age of five years.

15-16. *Could this be Autism* (pub. by The National Autistic Society)

17-18. *The Autistic Spectrum: a guide for professionals and parents* by L Wing.

19. For further information see page 30

The Autistic Spectrum: a guide for professionals and parents by Lorna Wing (pub. Constable).

20. For further information see page 21 and pages 110-119 of *The World of the Autistic Child* by Bryna Siegel (pub. Oxford University Press)

21-24. *The Autistic Spectrum: a guide for professionals and parents* by L Wing

25. *Could this be Autism* (pub. by The National Autistic Society).

26-27. *The Autistic Spectrum: a guide for professionals and parents* by L Wing

28. *Could this be Autism* (pub. by The National Autistic Society)

29. *The Autistic Spectrum: a guide for professionals and parents* by L Wing.

30. The National Autistic Society produce a booklet called *Managing Feeding Difficulties in Children with Autism.*

31. The author has also noted this in non-Autistic Spectrum Disorder children who have other conditions that are found within the SpLD Profile.

32-35. *The Autistic Spectrum: a guide for professionals and parents* by Lorna Wing (pub. Constable).

36. *The World of the Autistic Child* by Bryna Siegel (pub.Oxford University Press) looks in detail at the various factors which affect the parent's reaction to diagnosis.

37. This information is collated via checklists/rating scales; e.g. Autism Behaviour Checklist (ABC), Childhood Autism Rating Scale (CARS), Autism Diagnostic Interview-Revised (ADI-R). These correlate the information against the standardised criteria for autism as found in the DSM-IV or the ICD-10.

38. *The Autistic Spectrum: a guide for professionals and parents* by L Wing.

39. Assessment can be gained via a Local Authority. The National Autistic Society also runs its own assessment centre 'The Centre for Social and Communication Disorders' Tel: 0208 466 0098

40. The Local Educational Authority may have an expert on Autism who can advise on these; if one is not available then contact The National Autistic Society (page 43) and Afasic (page 63) for information on them.

CHAPTER 5
Co-morbidity and the complex profile

As the old Bible tale goes, if you build a house upon the sand it will fall. Only by providing good foundations can we hope for our house to stand tall and withstand life. Thus, if we do not enable those with the conditions within this book to stand tall then they are likely to drive educators to distraction, upset lessons and monopolise classrooms or (if a particular sub-group of Attention Deficits is present) they will sit in a corner and 'daydream' their life away.

Co-morbidity is the term used when there is more than one condition present, when this occurs the student has a complex profile. The case studies in this book show how common it is for professionals to miss the identifiers when a student has such a profile. In last few years many professionals have started to look further afield than their own speciality. This has resulted in a growing awareness that it is common for individuals to have more than one condition. For many individuals it is the issue of co-morbidity (and society's reaction to such a scenario) that causes them the most problems. Many professionals feel threatened by complex profiles. They feel threatened by the expertise of the adult who experiences them, or threatened by the expertise of the parent of the child who has them. Such adults and parents have little choice but to become their own experts as, all too often, such expertise is not available to them from the professionals around them. Some professionals possess great expertise and/or want to learn about the conditions found in this book, others do not. Professionals have a duty to update their knowledge - this is one of the duties of a doctor who is registered with the General Medical Council (see http://www.gmc-uk.org/standards/default.htm).

TAAO Profile
Individuals can have any combination of **T**ourette Syndrome, **A**utistic Spectrum Disorder and **A**ttention Deficit Hyperactivity Disorder (with or without hyperactivity). The cherry on the top of this cocktail of conditions may be **O**bsessive Compulsive Disorder in which the person's mind becomes locked into behaviours and thoughts (see page 71). Any combination of these will have a great impact upon individuals and their families throughout their lives, with those having a full **TAAO Profile** needing a huge amount of support from professionals and family members.

SLAAMS Profile
This is characterised by difficulties in the five areas of **S**peech, **L**anguage, **A**uditory processing, **A**ttention and **M**otor **S**kills (which may be accompanied by some features of Asperger's Syndrome). This profile is discussed in Book 3.

Multi-disciplinary (multi-agency) assessment and support
Individuals with complex profiles are likely to need an advocate from late teens onwards (see page 33) and assessment by a wide range of professionals (e.g. medical, educational and social services). They, and their families, will need a great deal of support from the professionals - in some cases this does occur but all too often this does not happen.

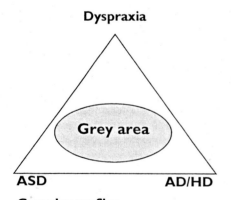

Dypraxia

Grey area

ASD   AD/HD

Complex profiles
Various ones exist some of which already have names; e.g. DAMP Syndrome (see page 48) whilst other patterns (such as a TAAO Profile) exist but are, as yet, unnamed.
DAA Profile
Some students fall into the 'grey area' shown above. They do not meet sufficient criteria for any of the conditions and often no provision is made at all for their difficulties even though it may be much needed.

CHAPTER 6
Asperger's Syndrome
Please read Chapter 4 before reading this chapter.

Asperger's Syndrome

(In this book, Asperger's Syndrome has been spelt with an apostrophe, following the style of Tony Attwood. Asperger's Syndrome is named after Hans Asperger; he lived in Austria and his paper describing the condition was published in 1944 (whilst Leo Kanner's paper on autism was published in USA in 1943).

Each person who has this condition will have the characteristics shown on pages 46-47 but there will be big variations between individuals as to which features will be more noticeable than others. The presence of better language skills (as compared to those individuals who have classical autism) may mean that the condition remains undiagnosed for a long time, possibly until the individual's teens or adulthood. The individual may also have other conditions that are found within the Specific Learning Difficulties Profile (for example, Dyspraxia/DCD), which may mask the indicators of Asperger's Syndrome. This late recognition can cause considerable problems for the individual, including developing emotional and behavioural problems as a result of being bullied and teased by other children who find the 'difference' in his/her behaviour offensive and/or upsetting. Lack of recognition results in a failure to meet the individual's needs and his/her parents may blame themselves (or the child/adult) for their unusual behaviour.

Once recognised, there are few facilities available for this group at present. Some children will be in mainstream school whilst others will be in specialist schools for children with autism, learning disabilities, or, a school catering solely for children with Asperger's Syndrome (contact one of the Autistic Spectrum Disorder charities for guidance - see page 43). Academic progress will depend upon the support and encouragement of parents, carers and educators. If adequate provision is not made, these children may become isolated, distressed and depressed in adulthood because they find it so hard to make friends. (See page 10) However, adults can go on to live fulfilling lives, attend further education (including university) go into employment and develop friendships. They may also be able to live independently, or near their families. Asperger's Syndrome has the following set of characteristics:

General

▸▸ there may have been difficulties during birth.

▸▸ a dislike of changes in routine (can find changes in school/work/ timetable/change of staff upsetting and difficult to cope with).

▸▸ likely to have difficulties in learning by observation.

▸▸ likely to have problems in working as part of a team.

Case study: Adult with Asperger's Syndrome and Dyspraxia

My eye contact is there but that does not mean that I understand the non-verbal messages. I pretend to maintain eye contact but when I do so it feels as though someone is poking a needle in my eye and my eyes just hurt with the intensity of eye contact.'

'If I drive a car straight on a road, I got really anxious if cars pulled out of the side road, it was the unpredictable nature of driving on the road that really made me anxious. If road works blocked my normal route, I used to just wish that I could leave the car and walk away. I couldn't change lanes at the last minute, I needed to be told well in advance. I just used to get fixed onto one issue and wouldn't let it go.

In my job I had to role play, I was terrified of role plays, sometimes I just wouldn't turn up.

Identification Solutions for Behaviour by Jan Poustie   ISBN 1 901544 82 6

What's the difference?
It is important that individuals (and their families) are referred to the correct specialist. The differences between the different professionals that the child, parents and adults come across are not always realised. Thus it may not be realised that when dealing with emotional problems psychiatrists may have a tendency to want to make a diagnosis whilst clinical psychologists may be less concerned about diagnosis and tend to think more about the psychological aspects of a condition. For an explanation of roles (and areas covered by) the different professionals that one is likely to come across see page 71.

▸▸ an awareness that they are 'different' from their peer group and distress because of this (such awareness is heightened in their teens and early adulthood).

▸▸ The individual has unusual interests, in which the individual becomes deeply engrossed and which usually involve classifying information and exceptional memory skills, for example lists of dates.

Intellect and academic skills

▸▸ average (or above average) intelligence.

▸▸ similar levels of non-verbal and verbal functioning.

▸▸ often excelling at learning facts and figures.

▸▸ difficulties in thinking in abstract ways (this causes difficulties in various subjects, such as creative writing in English, religious education and literature).

▸▸ original and creative thought patterns.

Social skills

▸▸ may try to be sociable (but peers tend to avoid them because of their apparently eccentric behaviour)

▸▸ may be the subject of teasing and/or bullying. (Bullying can also occur with Dyslexia - Book 4, Dyspraxia/DCD - Book 6, Auditory Processing Disorder - Book 3, Attention Deficit Disorder - Chapters 2 and 3, Tourette Syndrome - Chapters 1and 7 and Specific Language Impairment - Book 3)

▸▸ difficulties in making and maintaining relationships.

▸▸ may become more isolated and obsessional as they get older.

▸▸ difficulties in understanding how other people think.

▸▸ may develop anti-social behaviour (may be violent to and/or threaten others).

Movement

▸▸ may exhibit repetitive movements, for example, swaying and rocking.

▸▸ may develop unusual postures.

Language Development

▸▸ fairly normal early development.

▸▸ may speak very fluently.

▸▸ failure to make adjustments in their use of language to fit different social contexts or the needs of their listeners

▸▸ likely to have problems in expressing themselves, for example via facial expressions, gestures or posture.

▸▸ may have semantic-pragmatic disorder or higher level language disorder (see Book 3).

Case study: Paul
Paul has Asperger's Syndrome, it was diagnosed when he was four years old but, like many other students, the diagnosis did not come easily. The mother had to persuade the paediatrician (and the child psychologist) of the extent of his difficulties. (She took along to the meeting the Health

Visitor and the nursery nurse from the special needs nursery.) Paul is atypical, in that he is very sociable, is interested in people and relationships, watches sitcoms and uses them to help him understand how people behave. He is very good at expressing his feelings, has a great deal of tact and understands other people's feelings. When at nursery his inappropriate hugs of girls was the first indication that his social behaviour was not normal. At age thirteen, he works to a slightly reduced timetable, no longer studying art or classics. The former was dropped because his visual perceptual and fine-motor skills were poor; classics was dropped because the homework was arts-based and so depended upon good fine-motor skills. Gross-motor skills, gauging the speed of moving vehicles, and catching and throwing are still weak. Paul's mother has taught him a strategy of using the number of trees lining the road in relation to an approaching car as a way of gauging its speed. She took him to various streets and together they worked out safe strategies; for example, if you cross here and the car is at that tree you will have time to cross the road safely.

When he was assessed at age twelve by a paediatric occupational therapist he was found to have all of his motor skills below the first percentile (extremely poor); his spatial skills were also extremely weak, though his judgement of colour and alignment of items is excellent. His mother has noted that he still moves very slowly when going up/down stairs. Although there are language problems, in that he has a problem in creating sentences, he does seem to have a flair for learning foreign languages. Paul's case shows us is that we cannot judge all those students who have a condition as being or behaving the same. Each will be different but all will share some of the characteristics of the condition.

Case study: Richard
Richard has Asperger's Syndrome and Tourette Syndrome. Richard's mother contacted the authoress in the autumn of 2000. She was extremely concerned regarding the functioning of her son who was aged eight years. She had taken him out of school because he found it so stressful. Although Richard had been on the Special Needs register for the first two years of school (because of his fear of going to school) no attempt had been made to assess him and no conditions had been identified. There had been a history of food intolerances, behaviour and social skill problems and learning and motor coordination difficulties, attention deficits and tics (see pages 1-2). There is evidence that those with autism are more likely to have allergies, asthma, selective IgA deficiency including elevated serum IgG (see www.autism.com/ari/dan.html). A blood test conducted in America showed that Richard had this profile. The authoress had several long telephone discussions with the

Despite his motor difficulties, Paul has learnt to play the violin and this has helped his academic functioning. He has obtained his Grade 2 in this instrument (for information on how music can improve learning functioning see Book 3 and *Music Solutions for Specific Learning Difficulties* by Jan Poustie).

Motor coordination difficulties may be seen
Individuals with Asperger's Syndrome may:
▸▸ be clumsy (may have difficulties in learning certain motor skills e.g. learning to ride a bike and to swim) see Book 6 - Dyspraxia/DCD).
▸▸ have motor coordination difficulties, Attention (see Chapters 2 and 3) and perception difficulties present. People with this pattern of difficulties may be defined as having DAMP Syndrome (see Book 6 - Table 1)

READING

📖 *The Curious Incident of the dog in the night-time* by Mark Haddon. ISBN 0099450259. This brilliant novel, written from the perspective of a teenager who has Asperger's Syndrome is a must read for anyone who wants to gain an understanding of this condition.

📖 *Asperger's Syndrome - A Guide for Parents and Professionals* by Tony Attwood: Jessica Kingsley Publishers ISBN 1-853025-77-1 This easy-to-understand book is definitely the first book to read if you want to explore the subject of Asperger's Syndrome.

📖 *Autism and Asperger Syndrome*, edited by Uta Frith (ISBN 0 521 38608 X), published by Cambridge University Press. This excellent book provides a translation of Hans Asperger's 1944 paper in which he first describes the syndrome. It is a fascinating read.

📖 *A Martian in the Playground*, published by Lucky Duck Publishing, Bristol. Provides a first-hand account of what it was like to grow up having Asperger's Syndrome.

📖 *Children with Autism and Asperger Syndrome: A guide for practitioners*, (ISBN 0 471 98328 4), by Patrica Howlin, published by John Wiley & Sons, Chichester, UK.

📖 *Eating an Artichoke - A Mothers perspective on Asperger's syndrome* - Echo J. Fling ISBN 1-85302-711-1 Jessica Kingsley Publishers

📖 *Asperger Syndrome - A Practical Guide for Teachers* - Cumine, Leach & Stevenson: David Fulton Publishers ISBN 1-853464-99-6.

See pages 38 and 44 for other useful titles.

mother. As a result of these she asked the mother to look up Tourette Syndrome on the internet and to fill in Tony Attwood's Asperger's Syndrome checklist. (For information on Tourette Syndrome see Chapters 1 and 7.) The author also advised the mother that Developmental Dyspraxia and Specific Language Impairment also seemed likely. Further discussion with the mother (and the studying of the extensive case history notes provided by her) resulted in the author producing a written report as a basis for a referral for a multidisciplinary assessment. This encouraged the mother to ask her GP to refer Richard to a consultant paediatrician. In May 2001 Richard received a diagnosis of Tourette Syndrome and Asperger's Syndrome. Weak receptive language (see page vi) and formulation of sentence skills were also confirmed. Further assessments were then going to be made (i.e. motor coordination and educational psychologist assessments).

Richard's language assessment reveals the problems that he experienced in the school setting. He was able to formulate (create sentences) but took a long time over each one. He was unable to use picture clues when creating the sentences (he could only use the information within his own mind). Being only able to work to one's own agenda is typical of those who have autism. Richard may also have had problems trying to cope with integrating auditory and visual stimuli for he closed his eyes in order to work out his sentences. His difficulties in understanding spoken language would have caused him problems in any learning and social environment. His mother continues to educate him at home. It looks as though she will do so for the foreseeable future as Richard becomes distressed whenever he thinks of school. His mother comments:

> As the diagnosis has evolved I have gradually been able both to understand him better and to help him more. I find that I can accept his problems more, I understand that his difficulties are fundamental problems and not him being bloody-minded.

Richard has found a brilliant solution to the problem of becoming distressed whenever he gets something wrong. Now, his mother asks questions not of Richard but of his toy animals. If the animal gets it wrong it is 'the weakest link' and gets voted off the team. So far, the fox remains the champion!

Referring, Help and Support

Referral is made in the same way as for Autistic Spectrum Disorder (see Chapter 3). Use the Australian Scale for Asperger's Syndrome checklist when making a referral (see PIC 9 pages 60-62 or go to: www.tonyattwood.com). Details of the DSM IV Diagnostic Criteria for Asperger's Syndrome can be found at: www.ummed.edu/pub/o/ozbayrak/aspcrit.html. See page 43 for Help and Support.

CHAPTER 7
PANDAS

PANDAS (Paediatric Autoimmune Neuropsychiatric Disorders Associated with Streptococcal infections) is a newly recognised group of disorders, which are due to basal ganglia dysfunction in the brain. They were first described in 1998. Although, by definition they are meant to be a purely paediatric condition, adult cases have been identified. PANDAS is a spectrum of disorders with the majority presenting with a tic disorder not too dissimilar to Tourette Syndrome (TS) and/or an Obsessive Compulsive Disorder (OCD). In reality, most patients with PANDAS have both a tic and obsessive compulsive disorder. Like TS, there also appears to be a genetic predisposition to PANDAS, with many individuals having a positive family history of a similar disorder in that:
- 50% have a 1st degree family member with psychiatric disease (e.g. parent or brother/sister),
- in approximately 30% of the cases post streptococcal autoimmunity is found of 1st/2nd family members (e.g. parent, brother/sister, uncle/aunt/cousin),

In summary approximately 60% will have a positive family history.

There is evidence which shows that the PANDAS hypothesis, i.e. basal ganglia dysfunction secondary to Streptococcal infection, is also implicated in subgroups of patients with Tourette Syndrome, ADHD or Obsessive Compulsive Disorder. Streptococcal infection appears to trigger an aberrant (abnormal) immune response that then reacts with the basal ganglia. The resultant inflammation in the basal ganglia, an area of the brain responsible for the control of movements, emotions and various other things, then manifests (shows itself) with abnormal movements and an emotional and behavioural disorder. So with basal ganglia malfunction we may see:

1. Unusual movements: e.g. any of the following:
   - abnormal excessive movements, e.g. chorea (rapid semi-purposeful movements), tics (rapid repetitive movements), dystonia (a fixed writhing movement and/or tics),
   - reduced movements, e.g. slow movements or Parkinsonism.
2. Psychiatric disturbances which affect mood and emotion; e.g. there can be any of the following:
   - anxiety,
   - obsessive-compulsive behaviour,
   - depression (there is now a well established link between anxiety and depression, see page 10 for details on depression),
   - Attention Deficit Disorder (with or without hyperactivity).

Case study: Louise (13 years old)
Louise has Asperger's Syndrome, ADHD, Tourette Syndrome (TS) and PANDAS. She is at a mainstream comprehensive school. She has had frequent streptococcal infections since the age of 13 months. Before she

Each streptococcal infection (e.g. pharyngitis or tonsillitis, which are throat infections) causes further problems. It is believed that with repeated attacks the dysfunction may become permanent. Treatment with antibiotics at onset of infection is essential in order to prevent the aberrant (abnormal) immune response and to try and prevent attacks. Whether or not long term use of antibiotics will prevent permanent brain damage has yet to be established. The criteria for diagnosing PANDAS are:
- Presence of OCD and/or tic disorder,
- Prepubertal onset (e.g. happens before puberty)
- Episodic course of symptom severity (e.g. stronger symptoms appear at times),
- Association with neurological abnormalities,
- Temporal relationship between symptom exacerbations and streptococcal infections (e.g. a relationship can be seen between the infection happening and a worsening of the basal ganglia malfunctioning.)

Notes: For information relating to:
- OCD and basal ganglia dysfunction see page 71.
- PANDAS see ww.tourettesyndrome.net/ pandas diagnosis.htm

IEP (Individual Education Plan)

An IEP states the details of the student's education and the strategies, resources and professionals that will be used in order for the student to achieve short-term targets. According to the Special Educational Needs Code of Practice, (ref: DfES/ 581/2001) which LEAs must not ignore and Sections 4 and 5 of the SEN Toolkit (ref: DfES 558/2001) which accompanies it:

- an IEP should be written in consultation (and agreed whenever possible) with both parent and child.
- The child should be involved in setting their own targets and in agreeing/ implementing appropriate strategies.

Transition Plan

This is recommended in the Special Educational Needs Code of Practice for statemented children. However, with the culture in the UK of less and less statements being issued it is also necessary for non-statemented students who have significant difficulties to be provided with Transition Plans. It will be vital that a Transition Plan is created by Louise' school in Year 9 to work out with the parents, and other agencies (including Connexions), a way for Louise to access education once she is 16 years old. Connexions (which provide career's advice and advice on post 16 education) have special advisors for students who have special needs. *Free copies of the documents mentioned above are available from: Tel: 0845 6022260.*

Case study: Louise

Louise's view: *'I want school to stop people bullying me. The fact that people stare at me is the most annoying thing, we park in disabled lots and people stare at us because they think we're not disabled.'*

Dad's view: *'We daren't promise anything because if we can't keep it hell breaks out, so it's impossible to change plans at short notice, we live on guilt.'*

was 12 years old she was diagnosed as having ADHD and Asperger's Syndrome. At 12 years old she was diagnosed as having TS. For years her parents requested that IEPs and a statement be raised for Louise. A few months ago Louise was awarded a statement that provides her with full time one-to-one ancillary help. At the same time, her parents found out that an IEP existed but they had never seen it or been aware of its existence! Schools and LEAs who fail to properly involve the parent/ student when raising IEPs (and/or who fail to raise IEPs in the first place) cannot expect parents to trust the educational provider.

TS started when she was 11 years old with small tics and mouse squeaks which everyone ignored. Louise comes into the PANDAS group with TS. In 2002, a couple of days after a sore throat the tics exploded overnight into full blown TS, huge gross motor tics, flailing limbs which continued all day, screaming and screeching, honking like a goose, making parakeet noises. There was a new tic every day. The parents were in shock, The GP's reaction *'I'm out of my league here'*, He gave Diazepam to settle her as a first aid measure. Louise was already under a paediatrician for her other conditions so mum rang and she saw Louise within three days. She prescribed Haloperidol but after three tablets Louise had a massive reaction to it that was more scary than what had happened before. This resulted in her being in hospital for two days with the following: navy blue tongue stuck out of mouth, lockjaw, saliva just pouring out of mouth. They gave her a large dose of diazepam; Mum, who is a nurse, was very concerned as she realised that this was very serious. Now the paediatrician admitted that she was out of her league. Although Louise was not in school for three months due to the severity of her symptoms her school maintained the contact. (The school is expected to do this under the *Access* document, see page 54.) However, no NHS support for the parents existed during these three months. They were told that it would be 6-9 months before Louise could see a specialist for TS. Mum's comments:

'The present situation is that neither set of grandparents really understand the situation, and find it hard to accept the problems we encounter. It has become a bit easier now we have the PANDAS diagnosis as it has a 'medical' cause and not a 'psychiatric' one. They think she tics for attention, and so do some of the other children at school.

She is on several medications, some for the tics and some for the ADHD (Ritalin and Concerta). The Concerta has helped a lot, its better than Ritalin – it makes everything easier, she only has to take it once a day, we find she concentrates better with the Concerta but it runs out when she comes home from school. So we can have wild tiger at the end of the day. We don't have a social life anymore. We have been out once together as a couple in the past year. We never know what the day is going to be like – it may be a really good day, it may be horrendous. We need educators to listen to us.

A major problem we are having at the current time is School Phobia - it is very difficult to get Louise to school in the morning. We feel like a rung out rag once we have managed to get her to school, and that is the days when we do actually manage to get her there at all. Then the teachers have a problem getting her to lessons. She just refuses to go. We are all hoping that the statement will help with this problem. The SENCO at school has estimated that she has lost at least 25% of the work this school year.

CHAPTER 8
Changing the future

We need to change the future if we are to:
1. halt the rapid rise in the number of students being seen with behavioural difficulties in our educational establishments;
2. provide appropriately for those who have the conditions in this book.

So, in order to change the future it is necessary for there to be a change in knowledge of, and attitudes towards, the conditions.

1. Causes of the rise in behavioural difficulties

When the authoress first started teaching in the early 1970s she never knowingly met an ADHD, ASD or Tourette Syndrome child. Yes, there were behavioural difficulties; in her first primary school one had to teach some of the children to use the toilet and not do it against the school wall. Yes, things were stolen (her classroom newt - it nearly suffocated in the culprit's pocket). At her first secondary school one dared not leave anything on the school walls as it would 'walk'. Yes, pupils did want to beat each other up in the classroom (fortunately, she managed to persuade the girl to change her mind) and there was glue sniffing, truanting and so on. The students swore at each other, but rarely at the teacher; behavioural problems have always been with us – but they were containable. So, what has changed?

The authoress started teaching in 1972 but it was not until the late 1980's that she saw her first ADHD child and saw an increase in asthma. In 1989, upon entering primary school, her younger daughter's asthma inhaler was given to the teacher who put it with a couple of others that belonged to that class. Five years later, upon changing schools, the teacher pulled out a large drawer full of inhalers belonging to the class and added it into the pile! The huge increase in asthma may give us one clue as to why the numbers of children being identified as having ADD/ ADHD and ASD have increased so much. Recent research making a possible link with asthma and the gasses released in chlorinated swimming pools is the first clue - are things in our environment changing health and behaviour? It is becoming increasingly obvious that when looking at the causes of (and strategies for overcoming) behavioural difficulties, we need to consider many factors: e.g.

▸▸ infections such as the streptococcal ones that are linked to PANDAS,
▸▸ environmental factors such as diet (including water intake), chemicals and metals; including the consequences of the changes in the way that our food is (and the things in our environment are) produced, preserved and stored (see Chapter 2 and pages 31-32),
▸▸ non-realistic expectations of adults as to what is normal behaviour,
▸▸ the body's reaction to living with large amounts of electrical apparatus (see pages 67-68),
▸▸ the fact that few youngsters get the exercise that they need,
▸▸ the stress of living with rapid change in almost all areas of life,

Have we, like blinkered rats travelling along a maze, been so busy travelling along one path (that of diagnosis of the conditions in this book) that we have not thought to look at environmental factors (such as diet and pollution) which cause the behaviours (or worsen them). For evidence that junk food causes aggressive and other unwanted behaviours see page 201-205 of *Seeds of Deception* by Jeffery M Smith, ISBN 1903998417, pub. Green Books.

Looking at the wider picture, at the other conditions which have also increased in the UK during the past two decades, can be helpful here. The *Global Initiative for Asthma* report findings are worrying: almost a third of children aged 13 and 14 in Scotland, Wales and England report asthma symptoms - more than anywhere else in the world. A quarter of UK adults are affected by asthma to some degree (see http://news.bbc.co.uk/1/hi/health/3492731.stm

How to make complaints
Some students have been so badly treated that they/their parents want to make complaint about some of the professionals involved in their case. Complaint about education; e.g.:

▸▸ School: to headteacher, governors, then Local Education Authority (LEA) and then Local Government Ombudsman (LGO);

▸▸ LEA: to Head of Education Department, Department for Education of Skills, LGO.

▸▸ Teacher: General Teaching Council www.gtce.org.uk
(Also see *Provision for Specific Learning Difficulties* by Jan Poustie 1901544184.)

▸▸ Doctor: General Medical Council www.gmc-uk.org/standards/default.htm (which also contains a very useful list of the duties of a doctor).

Patient and Public Involvement (PPI) Forums
Many of us would like to see changes in the way that local health authorities deal with the conditions in this book (and changes in the interface between health, education and social services). PPI Forums are new statutory bodies whose role is to influence the design of, and access to NHS services, be proactive, make the views of patients and the public heard and look at health in its widest sense. Each local NHS Trust has its own PPI forum to monitor its work. Health authorities cannot ignore PPI forums. The forums are looking for members. To join Tel: 0845 120 7115. Ask to have the application form filled in over the phone then you don't have to fill it in!

▸▸ the amount of (and the consequences of the) stress being endured by the student, and all of the adults who come into contact with him/her (including educators), when inappropriate provision is made,

▸▸ the controversial area of vaccinations and autism (see pages 31, 32),

▸▸ Metabolic dysfunctioning of Essential Fatty Acids (EFAs) which causes the body to have problems in utilising the EFAs found in food (see Book 1). EFAs make up approximately 20% of the brain.

Educational establishments:

▸▸ cannot have both the profits from machines dispensing caffeine/sugar-laden drinks and snacks to their students (and their students encouraged to consume junk food by the adverts on their exercise books) and also expect to have good behaviour.

▸▸ need to make water accessible at all times. They need to ensure that students who access it during the school lunch are not seen as 'nerds' by their peers or 'lost money' from the caterers out to make a profit from our school dinners.

▸▸ cannot allow catering to be run by the cheapest provider whose bid was based on using heavily processed foods (these often have had the Essential Fatty Acids removed to increase shelf life).

2.   Attitudes
There are some excellent professionals who work in partnership, in a fully supportive way, with those who have these conditions (and their families). They are a shining example to us all of how we need to deal with these conditions and those affected by them. However, as many of the case studies in this book show, there are also professionals who lack the necessary knowledge and experience. Some respond by becoming informed about the conditions, others do not. Individuals who have these conditions are then regarded by their educational establishments as being disruptive, and by the professionals they meet as a nuisance. They, (and their family members) may then be bullied by the professionals around them. We can change the attitudes and behaviour of professionals by:

▸▸ providing information and giving an insight into the impact of the conditions (hence this book and the case studies within it).

▸▸ becoming active in our local communities, make changes within the way that our health service operates (e.g. by joining a PPI Forum).

▸▸ making complaint to a school (and its governors), those in charge of local health, education and social services (and their relevant government departments) and ultimately the Local Government Ombudsman, tribunals and the courts.

▸▸ organisations becoming instrumental in creating change. Primary Care Trusts (these include GP's, Community paediatricians) and the Acute Trusts (our NHS hospitals) should ensure that their health professionals have a level of expertise in these conditions so that Local Education Authorities/schools are advised appropriately. Social services departments should provide the respite care and family support that many of these families so desperately need.

Change is needed; each of us needs to play our part in making it happen so that there is a better future for all of us.

CHAPTER 9
Access to education for children and young people with medical needs

The presence of the conditions found within this book cause many problems in the educational environment and as a consequence for far too many of these students (and their parents), school becomes a place of embarrassment, humiliation and distress. As a result of this students will have limited attendance at school or may no longer be able to cope with going into school. Some parents may opt out of the state system and home educate their children themselves (see Appendix 2) whilst others will be educated for a period of time via the Local Education Authority's (LEA's) home tuition system. *Access to education for children and young people with medical needs* (DfES statutory guidance document, issued November 2001) states various items that schools and LEAs must and should do, including that:

'An LEA must have regard to guidance given from time to time by the Secretary of State. This is such guidance.' (paragraph 1.0)

'Access' was issued to protect our most vulnerable group of students.

'this guidance sets out minimum national standards for the education of children who are unable to attend school because of medical needs.' (Introduction)

'This guidance applies equally to all those pupils who are unable to attend school because of medical needs, both those who are physically ill or injured and those with mental health problems.' (paragraph 1.1)

'Access' applies to those with school phobia, all students who are unable to go into their school for more than 15 working days and pupils who have an illness/diagnosis which indicates prolonged or recurring periods of absence from school; e.g. those with chronic illness who regularly miss some school.

There is evidence which shows that some schools and LEAs are ignoring important parts of 'Access'; this reflects a complacency within the UK education system that is quite appalling. What is believed to be the first Local Government Ombudsman (LGO) investigation into a complaint against an LEA and school concerning failure to implement the 'Access' document has recently been initiated (for how to complain see page 53). For free copies of 'Access', Tel: 0845 6022260, quote reference number DfES 0732/2001, or go to http://www.dfes.gov.uk/sickchildren Get the 48 page booklet not the smaller leaflet which goes under the same name.

Note: LEAs are empowered to provide for young people up to age 19 years if the usual post-16 providers (e.g. colleges) cannot provide appropriately for the student. The Learning Skills Council (LSC), provides special funding for this group of students. The LSC also has a contingency fund for special cases where there is dispute or uncertainty regarding the student's provision (Tel: 0845 0194170).

Consent
Some students receive tuition via their Local Education Authority (LEA) after they are 16 because of medical conditions which are present. LEAs need to be aware that 16 and 17 year olds are presumed in law to be competent to give consent for themselves for their own medical treatment and associated procedures. (So, if a signature on a consent form is necessary they can sign for themselves.) For further information, including the definition of 'competency' get a free copy of *Seeking consent: working with children* ref. 25752, from the Department of Health, Tel: 08701 555 455 or www.doh.gov.uk/consent)

Case study: Kyra (age 15)
A student can be declared competent prior to age 16. Kyra, a disabled student, was registered with a school and was also under an LEA home tuition service. She was not being allowed to study GCSE music. Kyra submitted a video and a letter to the Special Educational Needs and Disability Tribunal (SENDIST) advising them of her views and of how she managed her medical condition. The tribunal decision (February 2003) stated: *'We took the view that whether or not X takes exams, very much depends on her health and her views, and is something that ought to be decided by her.'*

The conditions within this book are very demanding upon professionals. They require that professionals understand, listen, support and provide. Failure to rise to this challenge results in a worsening situation where there are huge levels of conflict. This can only be resolved by these professionals becoming better informed — for only by improving the situation of those who have the conditions can they hope to improve their own.

Perhaps, for all of those involved in the conditions found within this book (professionals, adults, parents and their children) the old saying 'divided we fall, united we stand' is never more true. The 'road' we have to travel when these conditions are present may not be a smooth one but by working together, and supporting each other, it can be made a lot less bumpy and much more pleasant to travel along.

Conclusion

The presence of the conditions mentioned within this book make huge demands upon carers, professionals and the person who has the condition too. Early recognition and diagnosis is vital: it enables early effective intervention and management of the conditions, which, in consequence, will result in either fewer and less severe symptoms and/or in the symptoms having less of an impact on life. Even once diagnosed, individuals who have these conditions place extraordinary demands upon parenting skills, marital relationships, brothers and sisters, educators and all the other professionals who become involved. The family can find the behaviour of the individual so embarrassing that both child and parents become isolated. For some, events such as family trips (and using baby-sitters so that the parents can have time to themselves) are rare or do not occur. Educators who lack knowledge of effective management techniques can find that managing the behaviour of the student takes so much time that they feel the rest of the class is 'losing out'. Other professionals, such as GP's, social workers and paediatricians, can feel overwhelmed by the complexity of profiles and totally out of their league. Help is at hand, through accessing the various organisations, websites and books recommended throughout this book; a huge amount of information on how to help and support those who have these conditions can be accessed.

Failure to meet the needs of those who have the conditions within this book results in life-long anxiety, low self-esteem, depression and lost life chances for both the individual and his/her family. This, in turn, leads to an impoverished society because all of its members have not been enabled to reach their potential. We can reduce the impact of the conditions but in order to do so we need to understand the whole of the individual's profile and its causes. Autistic Spectrum Disorder will always have a far-reaching impact upon the life of the individual but some, such as those with Asperger's Syndrome, may be able to live independent lives and have successful careers. The difficulties caused by Tourette Syndrome will always affect the person but with the right support individuals can blossom. ADHD makes it difficult to achieve but with the right mentoring and support individuals can prosper.

Those who have one, or more, of the conditions found within this book can thrive but in order to do so they (and their families) need the right environment. Like a delicate plant they can, with the correct support and understanding, be enabled to flourish - and we all have a duty to make that happen.

APPENDIX I
Poustie Identification Checklists
PIC 5, 6, 9 and
Tips for educators

Each PIC checklist explains which items should be used for which age group.
Always include a copy of the relevant PIC when making a referral.
School age children *(both primary and secondary children): use all the items.*
Pre-school (3 - 4 years) *use only the shaded items.*
Adults *use items marked # (or all items if stated to do so in the instructions on the checklist).*

Method of use for each of the PIC checklists:

1. Fill in the student's details at the top of the checklist.
2. Fill in the checklist. Each statement has a rating scale (the numbers in the right-hand column): 5= this happens a lot, 1= this happens rarely. In each question circle each element that is present; e.g. in question A5 in PIC 5-R if students avoids and is reluctant to do tasks then both 'avoid' and 'reluctant' should be circled.
3. Professionals (and interested parents) should follow the advice at the bottom of the relevant checklists as to which of the book/s in the library you should now read; e.g. PIC 5-R advises you that if you have ticked question A3 you should read Book 6 of the *Identification Solutions for Specific Learning Difficulties Library*. Each of the books in this library contain additional checklists plus a wider range of indicators including more detailed information of the indicators seen in pre-school children and adults.
4. Enter the score in the 'result's box. Circle yes or no (as appropriate) in the 'Results' and 'Is a referral advised' boxes.
5. Parents may now hand in the checklist to the SENCO/ AENCO of their child's school and/or to their GP. Always include a copy of the relevant PIC when making a referral.
6. If the student scores positively on the PIC checklist/s and his/her profile matches the information within the relevant books from this library it does not automatically mean that the student has the condition/s. However, there are indications that the condition/s are present and so a referral for a diagnostic assessment via the student's GP is recommended. If the majority of the statements on a checklist are ticked, then there is a strong possibility that the condition is present. In such cases it is always advised that provision within an educational and home setting should be put into place for the likely condition/s whilst awaiting for such an assessment to take place.

From birth to five years: children's developmental progress by Mary D Sheridan (ISBN 0415164583, pub. Routledge. It is an excellent and easy-to-understand book which provides information on the developmental stages of children. It covers social behaviour, play, vision, fine movements, hearing, speech, posture and large movements. The reader is advised to use this book along with the checklists in this section when making an identification of a child aged three to five years.

PIC 5 - R: Poustie Identification Checklist - Attention Deficits Hyperactivity Disorder (3 years to adult)

GENERAL INFORMATION			
Assessor:		Method of Assessment:	
Name of student	Date of Consultation	Student's age	Date of birth
Results: Number of items scoring between 2 and 6 points = Are the criteria on page 15-16 met or does the student's profile fit the information in Book 5? Yes/No			Is a referral advised: Yes/No

Each statement has a rating scale: 5= this happens a lot, 1= this happens rarely. Only tick those behaviours that are present.

All items apply to school age children. All items apply to adults except for B4. Shaded areas = may be seen from 3 years. # = carries on into adulthood.		1	2	3	4	5
Section A. ATTENTION DIFFICULTIES						
A1	Makes careless mistakes/does not give close attention to details. # *(May miss out numbers in sums, miss out letters in words, misread symbols etc.)*					
A2	Has difficulty concentrating on tasks or play activities *(though if interested in the task s/he may be able to concentrate for a long time and is likely to resent having to leave the task).* #					
A3	Does not seem to listen to what is being said to him or her. #					
A4	Is easily distracted by extraneous stimuli. # *(e.g. distracted by noises and movements within a classroom/nursery, the pictures on the wall, or even his/her own thoughts; also consider that sensory integration difficulties may be present.)*					
A5	Understands instructions but has difficulty in carrying them out. #					
A6	Avoids/dislikes/or is reluctant to do tasks, especially those that s/he finds boring, or that require sustained mental effort. *(If the task involves mental effort s/he is likely to work better in a quiet environment. A child may leave homework until the last minute and may need a parent to keep him/her company in order to do it. The child may need one-to-one attention in a classroom in order to start and finish tasks.)* #					
A7	Has difficulties in organising tasks and activities. # *(Will be present in the pre-school child but tends to be more easily spotted in the school child and adults.)*					
A8	Often loses things necessary for tasks or activities at school/home/work *(e.g. toys, pencils, books, mobile phones, books, important pieces of paper).* #					
A9	Engages in physically dangerous activities without considering possible consequences. *(This is not done to gain thrills but s/he appears to be unaware of the consequences of his/her actions; e.g. runs into the street without looking. Adults may be aware of the risks but ignore them.)* #					
A10	Forgets things when doing daily activities *(e.g. may forget to turn up for a lesson/meeting).* #					
A11	May have great difficulty in starting tasks. *(This can occur even though s/he knows, and accepts, that the task has to be done.)* #					
A12	Daydreams when s/he should be doing another task. #					
A13	Fails to finish tasks. *(May move from one uncompleted task to another. May be very keen to learn a skill; e.g. play a musical instrument but easily loses motivation to learn it unless the skill comes very easily to him/her.)* #					
A13	Exhibits anxiety. *(e.g. may be worried about not getting tasks done but still fail to do them. The child may be worried about getting told off in playgroup or in school; (e.g. told off about getting his/her work completed to the teacher's satisfaction.) The child's behaviour is his/her way of demonstrating the anxiety.)*#					

Identification Solutions for Behaviour by Jan Poustie   ISBN 1 901544 82 6

	1	2	3	4	5
Each statement has a rating scale: 5= this happens a lot, 1= this happens rarely. Only tick those behaviours that are present.					
All items may be seen in school age children and adults. Shaded areas = may be seen from 3 years. *# = carries on into adulthood.*					
Section B. HYPERACTIVITY and IMPULSIVITY					
HYPERACTIVITY					
B1 Fidgets with hands or feet and/or may squirm in seat. *(In adolescence and adulthood the student may feel restless instead or fiddle with hair etc..)* #					
B2 Has difficulty remaining seated when required to do so; *(e.g. in the classroom, at the dinner table; in adulthood this may show as feelings of restlessness).* #					
B3 Runs and/or climbs in situations where it is inappropriate to do so. *(Any of the following can be seen; inappropriate behaviours in school; e.g. may climb up the ropes in the gym whilst waiting for P.E. lesson to start. Toddlers may learn to climb before they can walk.. Young children may run without thought of danger or of the fact that their parents are now out of sight.)* #					
B4 Has difficulty playing (or taking part in a leisure activity) quietly. *(Parents, teachers and partners may find the student unrelaxing and noisy to be with, though in periods of great concentration these students may be very quiet.)* #					
B5 Has unusually high levels of activity *(e.g. like a clock-work toy with no off switch!)* #					
B6 Talks too much. *(This may be the student's way of expressing his/her thoughts as there can be an immaturity in the student's ability to internalise thoughts so they 'talk it through'.* #					
IMPULSIVITY					
B7 Blurts out the answers before questions have been completed. #					
B8 Has difficulty waiting for his/her turn, in games or other group situations. *(May push other children out of the way to get to a toy, may not see the need to queue, [adults may hate queuing]. May become very frustrated if s/he cannot say what s/he wants to say now. May become distressed/ angry if you postpone tasks and activities. May ignore/be unaware of the needs of others.)#*					
B9 Interrupts conversations and other people's activities. *(So, may barge his/her way across a board game that other children are playing. Both adults and children may interrupt conversations. Adults may interrupt a colleague in the middle of an explanation or the speaker at a lecture..)* #					

Scoring (for students of all ages):

Method 1: If:
- the rating is 2-5 for two or more elements from sections B or C (or three or more elements from section A) then read Books 1, 5 and 6.
- If after having read Books 1, 5 and 6 the student's profile fits both the presence of ADHD (and criteria 2, 3 and 4 are met from Method 2 below) then refer the student for assessment.

Method 2: If the following statements are true then you can refer for assessment (although it is strongly recommended that you also read Books 1, 5 and 6 as well):
1. 6 or more indicators in section A are ticked or 5 or more indicators in section B are ticked.
2. Some or all of these indicators have been present before the age of seven years.
3. The behaviours are seen in more than one setting (e.g. at school, at home, with the grandparents, with friends, at work, when involved in leisure activities outside of the home etc.)
4. The student's behaviours are affecting his/her social, academic functioning or his/her functioning at work (i.e. few friends, known by all but not a popular member of the class.)

Referral: This is usually made via the student's GP to the NHS professional in your area who specialises in ADHD:Note:
- If A3, A4 or A5 is present then read Book 3 plus complete the Auditory Processing Disorder checklist at the back of it.
- A4: sensory integration difficulties see Book 6.

PIC 6: Poustie Identification Checklist for Autistic Spectrum Disorder (3 years to adult)

GENERAL INFORMATION								
Assessor:				Method of Assessment:				
Name of student		Date of Consultation		Student's age		Date of birth		
Results: Number of items scoring between 2 and 6 points = Does the student's profile fit the information in Book 5? Yes/No						Is a referral advised: Yes/No		

Each statement has a rating scale: 5= this happens a lot, 1= this happens rarely. Only tick those behaviours that are present.

	ASD indicators change over time and may be less obvious in very structured settings and in adults/higher functioning students. Item B1 will always apply. Items B6 and C3 may apply to some pre-school students.	1	2	3	4	5
I	Repetitive behaviours/movements (e.g. spinning) may self-harm (e.g. head banging) rigid in activities (e.g. no changes can be made), obsessional interest in one topic or aspect of the topic. #					
A. Difficulties with social interaction						
AI	Often appears aloof and indifferent to other people. (Note: attachment may be shown to parents/carers, may enjoy certain forms of active physical contact). #					
A2	Accepts social contact but does so in a passive way. (May even show some signs of pleasure in this but does not makes spontaneous approaches.) #					
A2	Approaches other people in an odd, inappropriate, repetitive way. (Pays little/no attention to the responses of those s/he approaches.).#					
A3	Interactions may be inappropriately stilted and over formal with family/friends/strangers.#					
B. Difficulties with social communication (verbal and non-verbal)						
BI	Does not understand the social uses of (or find pleasure in) communication. (Some may have lots to say but they talk 'at' others and not 'with' them.) #					
B2	Does not understand that language is a tool for conveying information to others. (The person may be able to ask for his/her own needs but finds it hard to talk about feelings or thoughts.) #					
B3	Does not understand the emotions, ideas and beliefs of other people. (Is not able to see something from another person's point of view.) #					
B4	Difficulties in understanding (or giving) information via gestures, facial expressions or tone of voice. (May use gestures but these tend to be odd and inappropriate.)#					
B5	Literal use/understanding of language; (if you say 'its raining cats and dogs' will look for the animals!).#					
B6	Uses an idiosyncratic, pompous, choice of words and phrases. Content of speech will be limited. (May be fascinated with words but does not use his/her vocabulary when interacting socially.) #					
C. Difficulties with imagination (affects play, written work etc.)						
CI	Does not play imaginatively with objects or toys, or with other children or adults. (A child may appear to be playing imaginatively by copying story lines from favourite stories etc. Will not be able to pretend; e.g. cannot pretend that a paintbrush is a car and move it round a track.)					
C2	Tendency to focus on minor/trivial things around him/her or an element of a thing rather than the whole thing. (So, the younger student may focus on a ring rather than the person wearing it.) #					
C3	Misses the point of activities that involve words; e.g. social conversation, literature (especially fiction) and subtle verbal humour. #					
C4	Cannot use past and present events to predict consequences or as a basis for planning the future. #					

Scoring (for students of all ages): If the rating is 2-5 for one or more items in <u>each</u> of sections A, B and C then read
- Book 5, if the student's profile fits then refer (also read Book I).
- Read Books 3 and 5 if two or more elements of section B are ticked.
- Read Book 3 if C3 is ticked.
- If B3 or B4 is present, then read Book 5.

PIC 9: Poustie Identification Checklist for Asperger's Syndrome (5—11 years)

The Australian Scale (reproduced below and continued on pages 61 and 62) is taken from *Asperger's Syndrome - a guide for parents and professionals* by Tony Attwood who owns the copyright of it. It is reproduced with the kind permission of Jessica Kingsley Publishers. This scale is based on the formal diagnostic criteria, the research literature on associated features and extensive clinical experience. Each question or statement has a rating scale with 0 as the ordinary level expected of a child of that age, 1= rarely and 6 = frequently.

GENERAL INFORMATION

Assessor:	Method of Assessment:

Name of student	Date of consultation	Student's age	Date of birth

Results (Number of items scoring between 2—6 points)	Is a referral advised: Yes/No

AUSTRALIAN SCALE FOR ASPERGER'S SYNDROME

A. SOCIAL AND EMOTIONAL ABILITIES

		0	1	2	3	4	5	6
1	Does the child lack an understanding of how to play with other children? For example, unaware of the unwritten rules of social play?							
2	When free to play with other children, such as school lunchtime, does the child avoid social contact with them? For example, finds a secluded place or goes to the library?							
3	Does the child appear unaware of social conventions or codes of conduct and make inappropriate actions and comments? For example, making a personal comment to someone but the child seems unaware how the comment could offend.							
4	Does the child lack empathy, i.e. the intuitive understanding of another person's feelings? For example, not realising an apology would help the other person feel better.							
5	Does the child seem to expect other people to know their thoughts, experiences and opinions? For example, not realising you could not know about something because you were not with the child at the time.							
6	Does the child need an excessive amount of reassurance, especially if things are changed or go wrong?							
7	Does the child lack subtlety in their expression of emotion? For example, the child shows distress or affection out of proportion to the situation.							
8	Does the child lack precision in their expression of emotion? For example, not understanding the levels of emotional expression appropriate for different people.							
9	Is the child not interested in participating in competitive sports, games and activities?							
10	Is the child *indifferent* to peer pressure? For example, does *not* follow the latest craze in toys or clothes.							

Identification Solutions for Behaviour by Jan Poustie   ISBN 1 901544 82 6

PIC 9: Poustie Identification Checklist for Asperger's Syndrome (5—11 years) continued

	AUSTRALIAN SCALE FOR ASPERGER'S SYNDROME cont'd							
B.	**COMMUNICATION SKILLS**							
		0	1	2	3	4	5	6
11	Does the child take a literal interpretation of comments? For example, is confused by phrases such as 'pull your socks up', 'looks can kill' or 'hop on the scales'.							
12	Does the child have an unusual tone of voice? For example, the child seems to have a 'foreign' accent or monotone that lacks emphasis on key words.							
13	When talking to the child does he or she appear uninterested in your side of the conversation? For example, not asking about or commenting on your thoughts or opinions on the topic.							
14	When in a conversation, does the child tend to use less eye contact than you would expect?							
15	Is the child's speech over-precise or pedantic? For example, talks in a formal way or like a walking dictionary.							
16	Does the child have problems in repairing a conversation? For example, when the child is confused, he or she does not ask for clarification but simply switches to a familiar topic, or takes ages to think of a reply.							
C.	**COGNITIVE SKILLS**							
17	Does the child read books primarily for information, not seeming to be interested in fictional works? For example, being an avid reader of encyclopaedias and science books but not keen on adventure stories.							
18	Does the child have an exceptional long-term memory for events and facts? For example, remembering the neighbour's car registration of several years ago, or clearly recalling scenes that happened many years ago.							
19	Does the child lack social imaginative play? For example, other children are not included in the child's imaginary games or the child is confused by the pretend games of other children.							
D.	**SPECIFIC INTERESTS**							
20	Is the child fascinated by a particular topic and avidly collects information or statistics on that interest? For example, the child becomes a walking encyclopaedia of knowledge on vehicles, maps or league tables.							
21	Does the child become unduly upset by changes in routine or expectation? For example, is distressed by going to school by a different route.							
22	Does the child develop elaborate routines or rituals that must be completed? For example, lining up toys before going to bed.							
E.	**MOVEMENT SKILLS**							
23	Does the child have poor motor coordination? For example, is not skilled at catching a ball.							
24	Does the child have an odd gait when running?							

Identification Solutions for Behaviour by Jan Poustie   ISBN 1 901544 82 6

PIC 9: Poustie Identification Checklist for Asperger's Syndrome (5—11 years) continued

	F. OTHER CHARACTERISTICS *For this section, tick whether the child has shown any of the following characteristics:*		

a	Unusual fear or distress due to:
	  ❑ Ordinary sounds, e.g. electrical appliances
	  ❑ Light touch on skin or scalp
	  ❑ Wearing particular items of clothing
	  ❑ Unexpected noises
	  ❑ Seeing certain objects
	  ❑ Noisy, crowded places, e.g. supermarkets
		Yes	No

b	A tendency to flap or rock when excited or distressed.		
c	A lack of sensitivity to low levels of pain.		
d	Late in acquiring speech.		
e	Unusual facial grimaces or tics.		

Scoring
In total (including the 5 elements of section F) there are 29 characteristics:
If the answer is yes to both of the following questions then there is a possibility that Asperger's Syndrome may be present and so a referral (via your GP) for a diagnostic assessment for this condition is desirable.
1. Is the answer yes to the majority of the questions in the scale?
2. Look at each of the items that you have checked as being present. Is the rating for each of these items between two and six (i.e. conspicuously above the normal range).

▸ Parents and professionals should be aware that even if the answer is yes to both of the above questions it does not automatically imply the child has Asperger's Syndrome.

Authoress' notes to Australian Scale for Asperger's Syndrome

Whilst waiting for a referral parents and professionals are recommended to:
▸ read *Asperger's Syndrome - a guide for parents and professionals* by Tony Attwood ISBN 1 85302 577, published by Jessica Kingsley Publishers, London,
▸ put into place the strategies Attwood recommends for each element of the scale that has been identified as being present.

Explanations
▸ Items Fb: for an explanation of these behaviours see page 39.
▸ Items Fe: for an explanation of these behaviours see Chapters 1 and 7.

If you have ticked:
▸ Any items in Section A then read the whole of this book and complete PIC 5 and PIC 6.
▸ Items A1, A7, D21 then read Book 6 and complete PIC 4 (in Books 2 and 6 of this library).
▸ Item C19 read the whole of this book and complete PIC 6.
▸ Any items in Section B read Book 3 and complete PIC 1 (in Book 2 and 3 of this library).
▸ Item Fe read the sections on Tourette Syndrome in this book (Chapters 1 and 7 and pages 48 and 71).

Help and Support agencies for each condition are found at the end of each chapter. The impact of undiagnosed or unprovided for learning difficulties can be great. There have been tragic cases of children committing suicide because of this (parents too may reach breaking point). Ideally the contact details of at least the first section below need to be on display where students and parents/spouses can see them.

Samaritans   General office: 10 The Grove, Slough, Berks, SL1 1QP. Tel. 01753 532713, Helpline: 08457 909090. Offers support to those in distress who feel suicidal or despairing, and who need to talk with someone.

Childline   Royal Mail Building, Studd Street, London, N1 0QW Tel. 0207 239 1000, Fax. 0207 239 1001 Free helpline for children in trouble or in danger.

Community Drug Project   9a Brockley Cross, Brockley, London, SE4 2AB. Tel. 0208 692 4975, Fax. 0208 692 9968. Provides support within Lewisham area and referral elsewhere.

Depression Alliance   38 Westminster Bridge Road, London, SE1 7JB. Tel. 0207 633 0557, Fax. 0207 633 0559. Publish booklets including *Depression in Children and Young People, Self Help* and *Student Survival*.

MIND   15–19 Broadway, London, E15 4BQ Tel. 0208 519 2122. Produces useful booklets that deal with stress and depression including *Understanding Childhood Stress* and *How to Recognise the Early Signs of Mental Distress*.

Anti-Bullying Campaign   185 Tower Bridge Road, London SE1 2UF. Tel/Fax. 0207 378 1446. This organisation provides advice, information, understanding and support to parents of bullied children and to children themselves.

BATIAS Advocacy Service   Tel. 01375 392253

Disability Advocacy Service   Contact: Shirley Gray or Rachel Griffiths Tel. 01273 720972.

David Shepherd Associates   Carsington, Derbyshire, Tel. 01629 540815 Specialists in Mental Health Law and Practice.

IPSEA (Independent Panel For Special Education Advice)   4 Ancient House Mews, Woodbridge, Suffolk IP12 1DH, Tel/Fax. 01394 380518, www.ipsea.org.uk Advice line is normally open: IPSEA advice line (Tel: 0800 018 4016) normally operates Monday 10-4, Tuesday-Thursday 10-4 and 7-9 and Friday 10-1. IPSEA guides parents through the assessment and tribunal procedures. It can represent parents at SEN tribunals.

Contact a family   170 Tottenham Court Road, London, W1P 0HA Tel. 0207 383 3555, Fax. 0207 383 0259. Provides support for families who care for children with disabilities and special needs. Publications include *Siblings and Special Needs* and *A Parent's Guide to Statements of Special Educational Needs in England and Wales.*

Dial UK   (Tel. 01302 310123)   May know of relevant local help and support contacts,

SKILL   (The National Bureau for Students with Disabilities). This has helpful general information, especially about allowances for disabled students. Tel: 0800 328 5050 (1.30–4.30 pm weekdays.) Fax: 020 7450 0650. Website: www.skill.org.uk

Terrence Higgins Trust Ltd.   52–54 Grays Inn Road, London, WC1X 8JU. Tel. 0207 831 0330, Helpline 0207 242 101 (12-10 pm, seven days per week). Provides information and support concerning AIDS.

OSTEOPATHY AND HOMEOPATHY

Both these professions can help students who have ADHD. Homeopathy can be helpful in some cases, especially with regard to stress, behaviour and poor sleep.

Osteopathic Centre for Children   Harcourt House, Cavendish Square, London, Tel: 020 7495 1231.

General Council and Register of Osteopaths   56 London Street, Reading, RG1 4SQ Tel: 01734 576585.

The Society of Homeopaths   4A Artizan Road, Northampton, NN1 4HU. Tel. 01604 621400, Fax. 01604 622622. Website: www.homepathy-soh.org Send a stamped addressed envelope (A5 size or bigger) for a list of qualified professional homeopaths and information leaflets. Some practices now run Paediatric clinics. Homeopathic treatments can be of great benefit to individuals whose SpLD causes them severe stress and anxiety/poor sleep.

HOME EDUCATION

Parents have the right to educate their children at home. **Education Otherwise**   Emergency helpline: 08700 7300074. Website: http://www.education-otherwise.org

OTHER ORGANISATIONS

Afasic   50-52 Great Sutton Street, London EC1V 0DJ Helpline: 0845 355 5577, website: www.afasic.org.uk Charity for children and young adults with communication impairments. Provides support for parents and professionals via helpline, publications and conferences.

Twins And Multiple Birth Association   17 Clevedon Green, South Littleton, Evesham, Worcestershire, WR11 5TY.

National Association for Gifted Children   Elder House. Milton Keynes Tel: 01908 673677 Fax. 01908 673679. Web: www.nagcbritain.org.uk Email: amazingchildren@nagcbritain.org.uk

The British Allergy Foundation   Deepdene House, 30 Bellgrove Road, Welling, Kent, DA16 3PY, Helpline. 0208 3038583, Tel. office: 0208 3038525, Fax. 0208 3038792. Web: www.allergyfoundation.com A friendly confidential service offering callers individual, up-to-date allergy advice and information. The foundation also publishes a quarterly newsletter, which contains lots of helpful information and tips. To receive this newsletter and become a member of the foundation send a cheque for £5.00, with your details, to the above address.

Tips for Educators

For the conditions under which page 64-65 may be photocopied see page 56.

Students with Attention Deficits, Autistic Spectrum Disorder (including Asperger's Syndrome) and Tourette Syndrome (TS)

Many professionals find students who have this group of conditions very demanding. The only way to reduce the stress, for student and educator alike, is for the educator to develop a positive attitude towards the condition by becoming better informed about it and modifying tasks and the environment:

1. In pastoral sessions with the whole class/school explain the behavioural conditions that are present in your school. Giving the student's peer group an understanding of the conditions means that there is a better chance that the student's behaviours will be accepted by peers and an understanding that some students in the school will need a different sort of provision/discipline than the other students.

2. Provide in-service training in the behavioral conditions for all staff who will come into contact with the student (including non-teaching staff). Have a simple guide to the conditions easily accessible to all staff. Senior staff provide some 'time out' for teaching staff who are dealing with students who have the conditions found within this book.

3. Place the student in the classroom in the least distracting location when expecting him/her to pay attention to the task/do written work. For example, it may be helpful to place his/her chair facing a blank wall, or to put barriers around the child's desk so that s/he cannot see other pupils/items on walls). Keep him/her away from distracting doors and windows.

4. The student with these conditions needs more structure and routine than other students the same age. Any technique or strategy which structures the student's attention and activity is likely to be helpful. Keep to the same routine each day/lesson as much as possible and warn the student in advance if routines are to be to changed.

5. For work that requires the student to stay seated, help the student get started with your individual attention and then check back often to see if the student is still on track.

6. Make frequent contact with the student during the day, by making eye contact, touching hand/desk, or speaking the student's name to get his/her attention. This helps to keep the student from getting distracted from what s/he is supposed to be doing. A useful strategy for young children is to put a plastic beaker on the child's desk and every time that you pass the child and s/he is on task you praise the child and put a counter in the beaker. At the end of the day the counters are added up and the child praised. (Remember to attach the beaker to the desk so that it will not go flying!)

7. Give the student extra time to complete work without criticism (do not make them stay in at break).

8. Use materials that provide organisation and cues to help the student stay on task; e.g. Mind Maps, Map Masters, charts, reminder notes, a list of events for the day. (Use clipart from the computer to make the pictures showing what will happen in each lesson/break etc.). Learning aids can be used that structure learning, like computers, tape recorders, etc. Plus enable the student to plan and organise tasks using planning tools that suit the student's learning style.

9. Break assignments down into small chunks, use short assignments/tasks, and space out the assignments/tasks throughout the day.

10. Try to ignore noises, movements that are made by the student involuntarily; e.g. tics (TS students). Students who tap (e.g. AD/HD) give something soft to tap as it makes less noise.

11. Most importantly, the student needs frequent feedback and lots of meaningful praise for his/her successes (though be aware that some students with more severe forms of Autistic Spectrum Disorder and ADHD are likely not to respond to praise). Encourage the student, whenever possible, to evaluate his/her own accomplishments and to take pride in his/her achievements. Provide feedback and praise for the parents too.

12. The learning materials used can be important in maintaining attention so the educator may need to change teaching style/teaching materials to suit the student. Relying purely on the spoken word to explain or instruct will only result in great frustration and stress for educator and student alike. Instead use visual materials and materials that the student can handle or a visual-tactile approach (in which verbal instructions are combined with demonstration).

13. Remove caffeine from the environment; this includes removing it from the school premises so caffeine drinks should not be sold at the school shop, canteen etc.

14. Listen to the parents/student - they may well be the experts rather than you.

15. Conduct a 'risk assessment', in partnership with medical professionals and parents/student, to work out together the activities/circumstances which are likely to cause the student difficulties. Work out together a variety of solutions to those difficulties. Make sure all supply staff are aware of both the difficulties and the solutions.

16. Use the information found in the books mentioned below, books/journals you have come across, conferences you have attended and the reports on the student to inform your practice. Don't just file it away and ignore it.

17. Be aware that complex profiles will often be evolving diagnoses that will refine as the student gets older. Thus some conditions may be 'masked' by the presence of others. Provide for what you see, what has already been diagnosed and what you and the parent/student suspect whilst waiting for the full diagnosis to occur.

18. Use traffic light cards so that the student can warn you when s/he is starting to struggle to cope. Cards are attached to each other and sit on student's desk, if green is on top s/he is okay, if amber is on top s/he is starting to struggle, if red is on top s/he needs help NOW!

19. Stress and anxiety will increase the unwanted behaviours. Be aware that these students are likely to have higher levels of anxiety than other students. Work out, in partnership with student and parents, the things that cause stress/anxiety to the student and reduce the causes of them as much as possible. Senior Management Team should provide respite for educators by regularly taking lessons (or a small group) which includes the student with the behavioral condition.

Recommended publications

📖 *Creative and Factual Writing Solutions* by Jan Poustie, Next Generation, ISBN 1901544 834. Provides a large number of simple solutions including photocopiable Map Masters to help students improve the content of their writing.

📖 *Planning and Organisation Solutions Revised Edition* by Jan Poustie, Next Generation, ISBN 1901544 834. Provides plenty of strategies to improve planning and organisation skills plus a bank of photocopiable planning tools.

📖 *Literacy Solutions* by Jan Poustie Next Generation, ISBN 1901544 834 1901544 206 contains a chapter on planning and organization strategies and one on Behaviour and Literacy.

ADHD students

➼ Change activities frequently for the ADHD child in order to change the child's posture. For example, alternate chair/floor, standing, group, and moving around types of activities throughout the day. Ignore the movements of the hyperactive child (whenever possible provide him/her with opportunities to get rid of pent up energy).

➼ Provide a checklist when s/he is doing an assignment of all the elements of the task (including planning and gathering resources and date by which each element has to be completed). Then there is a better chance that all parts of the assignment will be completed and that it won't be done at the last minute causing stress to all concerned.

➼ Collect a copy of each stage of the assignment/task. (Then you will have something to show for the student's work if in a moment of distress s/he throws the work away because it does not come up to the standard of the work that s/he has visualized in his/her mind.)

Recommended publications

📖 *Attention Deficit Hyperactivity Disorder* by Dr. P.V.F. Cosgrove (Consultant Child and Adolescent Psychiatrist)

📖 *Understanding Attention Deficit Disorder* by Dr. Christopher Green and Dr Kit Chee (Specialist paediatricians)

📖 *The Hidden Handicap* by Dr Gordon Serfontein (Paediatric neurologist)

📖 *All about ADD - understanding Attention Deficit Disorder* by Mark Selikowitz. pub. Oxford University Press.

Tourette Syndrome students

➼ In partnership with the student set up a system for dealing with the tics, including that s/he has a place to go to during a severe/prolonged tic episode.

➼ Arrange for a buddy to take notes (or for teacher to provide notes) for the student whilst s/he is out of the classroom.

The website http://www.vh.org/Patients/IHB/Psych/Tourette/Modifications.html#6 provides a wealth of information on the teaching of TS students. Covers: Material Presentation, Classroom Environment, Time Management/Transitions, Mathematics, Organization and Handwriting, Grading and Tests, Behaviour, Reading.

Recommended publications

📖 *Making allowances—personal accounts of Tourette Syndrome* compiled by Chris Mansley. A compelling read, which gives a very good insight into this complex condition.

📖 *Tourette Syndrome – A Practical Guide for Teachers, Parents and Carers* by Amber Carroll & Mary Robertson

Autistic Spectrum Disorder/Asperger's Syndrome students

➼ Do not expect student to work as part of a team.

➼ Reduce change in the task/environment to a minimum; if change cannot be avoided then prepare the student in advance.

➼ Provide plenty of visual cues as to what the schedule for the day is/the rules of the classroom.

➼ If language difficulties (and or mutism is present) use a visual system to enable the student to express choices.

➼ Use social stories to enable a better understanding of social situations.

Recommended publications

📖 *Solving Behavior Problems in Autism* by Linda Hodgdon, pub Quirk Roberts Publishing. ISBN 0961678623. This comprehensive, very sensible and easy to understand teaching manual contains a wealth of information. It explains why the behaviour occurs, what underlying principles need to be understood/planning needs to occur in order to deal with it and how the problem can be overcome.

📖 *Teaching Children with Autism to Mind-Read.* Howlin, Baron-Cohen & Hadwin : John Wiley & Sons Publishers ISBN 0-471976-23-7 Very easy to read and practical book. It explains the principles of 'Theory of Mind', Contains dozens of scenarios to teach an understanding of others minds / emotions. A free workbook is available from the publisher.

📖 *The New Social Story Book* - Carol Gray : Winslow ISBN 119-3495-98 Social stories are short pictorial stories which help the person understand social cues and information. Contains pre-written stories on various subjects, explains how such stories should be written.

📖 *Comic Strip Conversations* - Carol Gray : Winslow ISBN 119-3495-98 Uses stick men illustrations to show how a child is helped to express thoughts/feelings, also explains how conversations and interruptions work.

Intervention and resources for Attention Deficits

This section contains information from the AD/HD Family Support Group UK information pack. (this organization has now disbanded). To avoid confusion, the better known abbreviation ADHD has been used throughout this article including quotes from authors who have previously used the abbreviation ADD.

The person with ADHD tends to over, or under, react to their world in either behaviour, speech or both. Typically they are the children who at age eight may have a tantrum because the breakfast cereal has run out but the next minute can cope when the television breaks down in the middle of a programme. They can also over react when an event that they have looked forward to occurs (e.g. by becoming over excited) or is cancelled (e.g. by losing their temper). In speech they can gush and not know when to stop (or know when to stop but cannot think of a way to round off their conversation, so continue with it).

It is generally believed that a combination of interventions will be needed in order to enable the person to function effectively. There is a variety of suitable interventions which exist. They can be divided into two groups non-chemical interventions and chemical interventions. Within each group there is a variety of choices and among them are:

Non-chemical interventions which can help
Behavioural Modification: This a form of treatment which appears to be often recommended for children who have ADHD. It works on the theory that the child's behaviour can be improved if the parenting skills of the parents are improved. However, An ADHD child can make even the best of parents appear to lack good parenting skills. This can become apparent when the behaviour of the non-ADHD children within their family are observed.

In order to modify the child's behaviour the parents will need to work together and to have the 'patience of a saint'. Some people believe that this method can work in the short term but does not often work in the long term. Mark Selikowitz (*All about A.D.D.*, pub. Oxford University Press) provides a good deal of information on this form of intervention. Behavioural intervention is not likely to work by itself, usually this intervention will need to be supported by something else. In the USA and in Australia this 'something else' tends to be chemical intervention (to correct the chemical imbalance in the brain); e.g. Ritalin but this treatment is still not generally accepted in the UK . Sometimes other interventions can be used instead; e.g. homeopathy, osteopathy and diet.

Homeopathy: Adults can attend any registered homeopath, children will need to attend a homeopath who has a special interest in children. They are given a variety of treatments; e.g.
▸▸one tablet at a time (which lasts for about six weeks)

▸▸one tablet at the time of the appointment and other tablets which will be taken at certain points during the subsequent weeks
▸▸a liquid which they take a tiny amount of on a daily basis

Homeopathy can reduce the frequency of the behaviours; e.g.
▸▸reduce the number of tantrums
▸▸enable the individual to be more balanced within themselves (so that they no longer feel at war with themselves) and can stop the mind racing.

Osteopathy: Certain osteopaths specialise in osteopathy for children. Sometimes the child has had a difficult birth which has caused various stresses to remain within the body after the birth; e.g. cranial compression which is a pushing together of the bones of the skull. This can result in a variety of problems including frequent ear/sinus infections. Specialised osteopathy has been shown to be useful in helping the 'child to calm down, sleep better, sit still for longer periods, and therefore improve concentration and learning'. *Osteopathy for children* by Elizabeth Hayden, page 40 (Pub. Churchdown Osteopaths, Gloucester)

Diet: Some research has been (and is being conducted) into dietary supplements. Contact The Hyperactive Children's Support Group (Tel: 01903 725182) for up-to-date information on this.
▸▸ Many people's behaviour is affected when their blood sugar level becomes low because they are not eating regularly enough. Some people 'see saw' between having too low a level of sugar, then eat something very sweet and so have too much sugar - their behaviour also 'see saws'. Regular eating of starch based carbohydrates e.g. wholemeal bread, brown rice and spaghetti will stop this sugar imbalance.
▸▸ Some people are allergic to the ingredients in some of the common foods; e.g. chocolate, cola drinks and wheat. (Carob, available from health food shops, can be used as an alternative to chocolate.)
▸▸ In other cases the behaviour of the AD/HD child may worsen after taking certain foods but the food itself is not the cause of the original behaviours. Remove caffeine and from the diet and reduce the number of high sugar snacks.

Other factors which can cause or worsen attention deficit behaviours
Any, or all, of the following may be present:
1. Lack of knowledge and/or acceptance of normal child behaviour.
▸▸   The demands of home life (both parents working) and a national curriculum that must be

taught 'despite the children' may well be resulting in adults having raised expectations as to what is 'normal behaviour' within the home and academic setting. We do seem to forget sometimes that children are meant to behave childishly!

▸▸ <u>Children are actually meant to be disruptive</u> - how else can babies ensure their survival; that we will indeed feed them. Adults who expect a child (especially a boy) to sit quietly all day, not rush around, never be aggressive or anti-social and so on are not being realistic.

▸▸ <u>Lively and childish behaviour</u> can be very tiring for the adult carers especially since, in today's society, adults are so stressed and there are few opportunities for the child to safely charge around. Roads in the past were seen as play areas, large areas of 'scrubland' existed near housing where children could make 'dens' and explore (and we gave our children more independence as we were less afraid of them being molested).

▸▸ <u>The need for physical exercise</u>. Children used to walk to school but fears of them being attacked and busy schedules (especially of working mums) mean that only a few of even our primary aged children walk to school anymore. Some teachers are observing that reception children are even being brought to school in pushchairs because mums are too rushed or do not want to take the extra time that will be involved if the child walks. Physical activities in the form of PE and singing used to be daily activities in the primary classroom. Nowadays the only daily exercise the child may get is at playtime. However, if s/he misbehaves, is slow at completing work then s/he will be deprived of that by the teacher who keeps the student in as a punishment or in order to finish work. Enabling the student to visit a park, play on garden apparatus etc. before and after school can help.

Therefore, we will see an improvement in behaviours if the adults involved with the student :

▸▸ *become better informed as to what is and what is not normal (and attention deficit) behaviour ,*

▸▸ *enable the student to increase the amount of exercise s/he has in the normal school day*

▸▸ *do not keep the child in during breaks .*

2. The personalities of the adults around the student will determine what they regard as normal behaviour so some will find the lively mind of the very bright and/or attention deficit child a pleasure to deal with whilst others will become irritated by their interruptions and by their 'going off track' during discussions. This can result in one teacher thoroughly enjoying teaching the child and creating a good relationship with him/her whilst the next regards the student as a 'pain in the neck'. Similarly, the parents can have one view of the child and the class teacher another.

If the teacher does not get on with the child then provide the student with a different teacher whenever possible and provide a mentor (another adult) to whom the student can confide his/ her feelings about the teacher. The mentor can also help the student understand (and possibly reduce) the behaviours which trigger the teacher's dislike of him/her.

3. The environment may be too stimulating (e.g. too noisy, too much movement, too much display material on the wall). Many classroom walls, especially in primary school, are covered with bright, colourful and interesting material. If the classroom also has high noise levels and lots of children moving around, is it surprising that some children find it difficult to focus on their own work! The authoress was appalled a few years ago when being shown round a new primary school. The head teacher was proudly showing his early years' classrooms and explained that the 'quiet area' had been removed from the original plans as it was no longer needed!

ADD children need to have access to a 'safe quiet haven' where they can work undisturbed.

4. The regime used by the adults will influence the attention deficit behaviours. Thus the heavily structured regime of school may suit many ADHD students but will be very difficult to achieve within the family setting plus maintaining such a regime may be frustrating for all other family members.

Our attention deficit children need firm discipline where the outcome of behaviour is explained in the calmer moments of the school/home day. However, strong discipline which is imposed unfairly (or for which the child can so no reason) will only alienate the ADHD child.

5. Chemicals in the environment (both within and outside of the educational establishment) can affect behaviour.

Parents can easily avoid most modern heavily chemical based cleansers and air fresheners and opt for 'green' ones. It may be more difficult to persuade the school to change though.

6. Sensitivity to the school's (or the room's) location. Many of our schools are by busy main roads. Some people have been found to be affected by vehicle exhaust fumes causing a range of symptoms; e.g. headaches, and fatigue.

Issues of electromagnetic radiation (caused by electrical sub-stations/pylons are now coming to the fore. Recently one special needs teacher noted that the small room in which he and his students were being asked to work was separated from a 6000 volt electricity sub-station by only a thin wall. He found that the electromagnetic radiation from the sub-station messed up computer monitors in certain parts of the room. The levels of EM emissions were measured. as a result of his concern over the room. (Such emissions are invisible and, not surprisingly, given the electrical impulses that travel through our bodies, can affect humans.) The room was surveyed and the emissions were found to be so high that he and his students were moved to a different room. (Needless to say, as happens far too often in special needs, he was moved to a tiny room in a not much better location; e.g. by the toilets!)

EM radiation has been implicated in ME (chronic fatigue syndrome). Two major organisations (e.g. a large banking institution) in Washington USA actually shield sources of EM radiation, ensure that no staff are working close to them and have special plants around (e.g. spider plants and peace lily) which absorb some of the radiation. This does make one wonder whether we need to be a little more careful about where we site our schools and which rooms within them we should be working in.

Recent concerns about mobile phone masts and the microwaves that they emit are now also raising concerns amongst some people. Also see Metabolic Dysfunction and other factors which can affect learning in Book I of this library.

7. Break assignments down into small chunks, use short assignments/tasks, and space out the assignments/tasks throughout the day. [1]

Attention Deficit coaching/mentoring

Both the teacher and the parents can help children who have ADHD to function more easily within their environment. Adults/older teenagers may need the help of a coach to keep themselves focused and balanced. ADHD coaches do not appear to be very common in the UK (the authoress does offer this service). The coach can:

- guide students through examinations; e.g. GCSE's where they can teach learning skills and keep the student on track,
- act as a non-involved 'sounding board' to enable students to know how their behaviour is being perceived
- act as a support to whom students can turn when they need it

How the parents can help

by AD/HD Parent Support Group UK - edited by Jan Poustie
(Note: much of the following applies to the educational setting too.)

No general plan can be applied to all such children and no one can make provision for every possible event in the home life of a child with ADHD. The clinician who advises the family needs to be fully aware of the various traits that the child displays. Systematic questionnaire data, interpreted carefully, can form the basis for a home management plan. The following general guidelines can also be helpful:-

1. Along with educational success, children with ADHD must have sufficient personal success in their lives. Their strengths must be recognised and used, even if the talents do not fit parental hopes or expectations. Artistic, athletic, or creative ability of any kind must be noticed and developed even if the child resists developing his/her strengths.

2. Children should not be expected to change behaviour

overnight. Parents should try not to use threats such as "if you ever do this again, you will be in big trouble." Instead, they should temper criticism with praise each day. The goal should be to decrease progressively the frequency and severity of inappropriate behaviour.

3. Parents should not attempt to deal with all of the child's undesirable traits at the same time. They should select one or two traits that they feel are the most in need of careful management and work on these exclusively or primarily.

4. Every effort should be made to shape behaviours without seeking or expecting to destroy the presence of symptoms; e.g. The mother of a highly demanding and insatiable child could limit it by saying,
"You seem to want things all the time. It uses up all my energy and time. From now on, you write down in a notebook everything you need or want. [2] *Every afternoon from 5.00 until 5.15, I will sit and listen to you. These will be my 'office hours' to hear about all of the things you want or need. We can discuss them only at those times."*
(Note: this strategy will not work if the adult cannot keep to the scheduled times.)

5. Sleep problems need to be managed carefully. Children should not be made to feel guilty about having trouble falling asleep. As long as they bother no one else, they should be reassured that sleep is their own affair. If a lack of sleep interferes with school performance, medication to induce sounder sleep may be tried (contact your Doctor or Psychiatrist first), along with other measures, such as the use of white noise, afternoon naps, relaxation tapes, reading in bed, hot water bottles, persuading the family pet to sleep on the child's bed and electric blankets if the child will be safe using one. [3]

Homeopathic and herbal remedies can also help, such as avena sativa which is available from Helios Homeopathic Pharmacy, Tel: 01892 536393. Products containing Valerian and hops can also help.(You must consult a homeopath/herbalist as to the correct dosage and suitability of use for your child/yourself. They can be found attached to some GP practices or via your local telephone directory, also see page 63.)

6. Children with ADHD benefit from predictability and structure at home. [4] Distinct schedules for getting up in the morning, doing homework in the evening, and fulfilling daily obligations have a beneficial impact. These children should be expected to assume responsibilities in a predictable manner.

7. Both parents must have similar policies about reactions to the child's various actions. This requires considerable discussion and planning by the parents. [5]

8. Children with ADHD often have difficulty completing homework assignments. The following will help them to achieve such tasks:

- A pre-set routine for work which involves mental effort each evening (except weekends) helps establish good study habits. If they have no homework, these children should at least sit at a desk and work in a workbook or perform some other intellectual tasks such as reading or working on an educational computer program. Their siblings should be working at the same time.
- There should be no television or other distraction permitted during the set homework hours.
- Parents may wish to purchase a set of textbooks for home use so that the student can underline and make notes in the margin as s/he studies.
- Children with ADHD should not have their desks in their bedrooms. This is too distracting an environment - the bed is associated with sleep: wall hangings and other belongings are a constant temptation to daydream. Ideally, a desk should be situated in another room or children should be permitted to work on a kitchen or dining room table or even the floor.

Use of detention in school

Just as prison is likely to achieve very little unless the prisoner attends rehabilitation classes so detention sessions in school are likely to achieve very little too. Instead of detention sessions we need sessions in areas such as:

- anger management,
- social skill development,
- planning and organisation,
- assertiveness training,
- negotiation skills,
- understanding body language.*

The educator ticks the appropriate session/s (based on the reason/s for the detention). The student, as his/her detention, joins a a small group of other students with similar difficulties in order to work out strategies to work out the problem that caused the detention. This way detention would have a chance of achieving something other than the alienation of the student.

*Note: Some of these students get themselves into trouble as they use aggression because they do not know:

- how to negotiate,
- the difference between being assertive and being aggressive,
- the meaning of body language or the effect of their own body language on others.

Useful addresses

The Hyperactive Children's Support Group
71 Whyke Lane, Chichester, West Sussex. PO19 2LD
Tel & Fax: 01903 725182. Provides a Basic Introductory Pack.

Osteopathic Centre for Children
Harcourt House, Cavendish Square, London
Tel: 0171 4951231 Fax: 0171 4951232

General Council and Register of Osteopaths
56 London Street, Reading RG1 4SQ, Tel: 01734 576585

The Society of Homeopaths
2 Artizan Road, Northampton NN1 4AU
Tel: 01604 21400 Fax: 01604 22622

ADDISS (National Attention Deficit Disorder Information and Support Service) 10 Station Road, Mill Hill, London NW7 2JU
Tel: 020 8906 9068, Fax: 020 8959 0727

Jan Poustie conducts ADHD coaching and provides lectures on Attention Deficits from her consultancy which operates under the name of: Next Generation, 68 Hamilton Road, Taunton TA1 2ES. Tel/Fax: 01823 289559.

Using chemical intervention

The decision as to whether to use drugs (and which one to use) can only be made in consultation with a medical specialist. If the doctor regards it as appropriate s/he will recommend such intervention but only the parent (or the adult/child who has ADHD) can decide whether or not to use it. There seem to be two schools of thought on the use of such drugs in the UK - those who are totally against it and those who are totally for it. Like everything else in the field of the Specific Learning Difficulties Profile what will work for one person - in one situation, will not work for another person/family.

The AD/HD Family Support Group UK (which unfortunately has now been disbanded) used to produce various leaflets on the use of chemical intervention which explained that:

- the advantages of using them; e.g. improved concentration span, self control, reduction of hyperactivity, the child being happier, less chance of academic failure,
- a possible side effect is reduction in appetite,
- the importance of gradually increasing the dose and the fact that the chemical quickly passes through the body,
- that research appears to indicate that growth is not affected,
- that becoming addicted to the drugs does not appear to occur.

Several books have good sections that cover the advantages and disadvantages of using drugs; e.g.

- **Understanding Attention Deficit Disorder by Dr C. Green and Dr K Chee** ISBN 0 09 181700 5 *These authors are very keen on chemical intervention.*
- **You mean I'm not lazy, stupid or crazy by Kelly and Ramundo** ISBN 0 684 80116 7
This book deals with ADHD in adulthood. It explains in detail chemical intervention in adulthood and also covers a wide range of therapies that can be effective such as yoga, psychotherapies of many types, self help, assertiveness training, sensory integration, massage, meditation etc.
- **All About A.D.D. by Mark Selikowitz** ISBN 0 19 553684 3 *Has comprehensive information on the use of drugs - also gives details of various studies carried out on the effectiveness of the drugs for modifying behaviour and learning.*

Co-morbid Disorders

Professionals need to be aware that Oppositional Defiant Disorder and Conduct Disorder can be present alongside ADHD. If either of these conditions is suspected (or diagnosed) both educators and parents will need the support of specialists; e.g. their Local Educational Authority's behavioral support team and their local NHS child psychiatrist.

Oppositional Defiant Disorder

These students exhibit a pattern of negativistic, hostile and defiant behaviour. They frequently lose their temper, cause arguments with adults and defy or refuse to comply with adult requests. Sometimes this can include evasion tactics whereby they agree to do something and then avoid doing it—this can be exceptionally frustrating for the adults who work with them. Such students can be charming, appear to be willing and then fail utterly to start the task. Great patience is an essential requirement of their educators. (See page 22 for diagnostic criteria.)

Conduct Disorder

Students will show a repetitive and persistent pattern of behaviour whereby they do all or any of the following:
- violate the basic rights of others,
- violate major age-appropriate societal norms or rules.

These violations fall into the following four main groups:
1. Aggressive conduct where they cause or threaten physical harm to people or animals,
2. Non-aggressive conduct which results in property loss or damage,
3. Deceitfulness or theft,
4. Serious violation of rules

Three or more of these behaviours must have been present during the past 12 months (with at least one of these behaviours being present in the past 6 months). This condition may be easily missed in the educational setting since students tend to minimise their conduct problems and the educator (to whom the child is referred for misbehaviour; e.g. senior management team) may not have adequate knowledge (or supervision) of the student.

Such students tend to be aggressive, use weapons to inflict harm and may threaten, bully or intimidate others. Children with this disorder are likely to have started a pattern of behaviour before the age of 13 whereby they:
- stay out late at night despite their parents ordering them not to do so,
- truant from school (adults are likely to absent themselves from work for no good reason).

The disorder has three different levels of severity:
- mild; e.g. lying, truancy, staying out after dark without permission,
- Moderate: e.g. stealing without confronting a victim, vandalism,
- Severe: e.g. rape, physical cruelty, use of a weapon, stealing whilst confronting the victim, breaking and entering.

There are three sub-types of this disorder:

Childhood-Onset Type

The condition starts before age 10 years and it is usually males that have this sub-type. It is characterised as physical aggression towards others, disturbed peer relationships, may have had Oppositional Defiant Disorder during early childhood. Also likely to have:
- Attention-Deficit/Hyperactivity Disorder,
- persistent Conduct Disorder,
- Develop adult Antisocial Personality Disorder.

Adolescent-Onset Type

Condition starts after 10 years. Compared with Childhood-Onset Type students are less likely to display aggressive behaviours and have more normal peer group relationships (although they often show conduct problems when with others). Seen in both sexes.

Unspecified Onset

This diagnosis is given if the age at onset of Conduct Disorder is not known.

Footnotes:

1. Though if the child is a global/qualitative learner it is important to introduce the concept globally first. (For explanation of learning styles see: Creative and Factual Writing Solutions by Jan Poustie et al, Pub. Next Generation. ISBN 1 901544 389)

2. Children with literacy difficulties could use a tape recorder and/or a Mind Map instead of a notebook.

3. Story and music tapes can also be useful though it may be necessary to switch off the tape at a reasonable hour otherwise the child can want to listen to the end of it. A parent reading a book/magazine which the child finds boring such as the engine specification of cars can also work.. (Choose your book with care - the authoress tried this with car maintenance books, unfortunately she did not realise that her 1 year old daughter was a budding scientist so it made the mother feel sleepy and not the child!). A television in the bedroom can excite the child too much and there is the risk of the child watching totally unsuitable programmes..

4. This can be exceptionally difficult and frustrating for those parents who really dislike structure in their lives and they can resent the child because of the need of such a rigid lifestyle. It can sometimes be necessary to maintain the schedule even during the school holidays.

5. This can often be the cause of many family arguments when one parent wants to be much tougher with the child than the other. Relatives may be of little help here and may even cause more difficulties -expressions from mother-in-laws such as 'I never let you behave like that' are definitely not helpful!

Obsessive Compulsive Disorder (OCD)

OCD causes the person to have obsessive thoughts or behaviours. Tics and OCD occur together much more often when the OCD or tics begin during childhood. Depression and OCD often occur together in adults, and, less commonly, in children and adolescents.

'There is no single, proven cause of OCD. Research suggests that OCD involves problems in communication between the front part of the brain (the orbital cortex) and deeper structures (the basal ganglia). These brain structures use the chemical messenger serotonin. It is believed that insufficient levels of serotonin are prominently involved in OCD. Drugs that increase the brain concentration of serotonin often help improve OCD symptoms. Pictures of the brain at work also show that the brain circuits involved in OCD return toward normal in those who improve after taking a serotonin medication or receiving cognitive-behavioral psychotherapy.' (Extract from www.ocfoundation.org website, printed with their permission.)

Case study: John (continued from page 3)

John has Asperger's Syndrome, OCD, ADHD and Tourette Syndrome. John is frightened of everything and so he does not go out by himself. He constantly has obsessive thoughts (which are mainly morbid) this results in him not letting his mum go anywhere without him as he fears that she will die.

Mum's comments:

'He has too much empathy for everyone and becomes exceptionally distressed when someone else is distressed or if someone else has a problem or setback (e.g. if someone has merely just lost a game). He has been a school phobic all his life and this is now very severe. He is extremely distressed because of this as he desperately wants an education. He cries because he wants an education and cries because he doesn't want to go to school.'

School phobia is covered by the 'Access' document (it provides for such students to have education (1:1 or in small groups) via the LEA at home and/or in other settings. The authoress was appalled to find out that home tuition has not been provided for John and that no provision for education is being made for him unless he attends school. The 'Access' document is not being implemented here (see page 54).

Help, support and information

OCD Action, http://www.ocdaction.org.uk
Aberdeen Centre, 22 - 24 Highbury Grove, London, N5 2EA. Tel: 0207 226 4000, Fax: +44 (0) 207 288 0828
OCD Foundation: www.ocfoundation.org

The Difference between Psychiatrists, Psychologists and Psychotherapist.

PSYCHOLOGIST

Deals with how we learn, think, feel, behave and act towards each other.

Clinical Psychologist: specialist training in mental health problems; works with all ages and learning difficulties. Tends to concentrate on behavioural and emotional issues. Diagnose, assess, deal with depression, mental illness, childhood behaviour disorders, personal and family relationships, learning difficulties.

Child Psychologist: works with children and their families.

Educational Psychologist (EP): teacher who has had further training to become an EP; works with children and schools. Assesses mainly problems with learning and behaviour in school. Does not usually do therapy or see children outside of school.

Counselling Psychologist: helps client solve or manage their problems; e.g. relationships and living.

PSYCHIATRIST (referred to as Dr.)

A doctor (prescribes medication): deals with mental health (prevention, diagnosis and treatment of mental and emotional disorders); may have an area of special expertise. Works in a variety of settings (including family centres and homes.

Child and Adolescent Psychiatrist: deals with diagnosis and management of psychiatric disorders from infancy to mid-teens. Uses a wide range of therapies including medication and family therapy.

Learning Disability Psychiatrist: deals with assessment and treatment (and provides advice and education to parents/carers/professionals such as teachers) of emotional, behavioural and psychiatric disorders associated with learning disability (including Moderate Learning Difficulties, challenging behaviour and autism). Work in a various settings including the family home.

Community Mental Health Team (CMHT)
Psychiatrists may work as part of the CMHT which may include a Community Psychiatric Nurse (CPN) who specialises in mental health (assesses and treats people with mental health problems in the community.

PSYCHOTHERAPIST

Helps people overcome maladaptive habits and anxieties deals with talking treatments; e.g. cognitive-behavioural therapy (which deals with learned patterns of thought and ways of dealing with them) also looks at the whole situation within which the patient has the difficulties (e.g. the family).

Cognitive Therapist is someone who has been trained in the use of cognitive therapy, which is a form of psychotherapy. It is a way of helping people to cope with stress and emotional problems by talking about the connections between the way we think, how we feel and how we behave.

Attention Deficits
 see Attention Deficit
  Hyperactivity Disorder
Atypical autism 34
Auditory Processing
  Disorder (APD) also
  known as Central
  Auditory Processing
  Disorder (C/APD) vi, 11 38
 in relation to
  ADD/ADHD 20
  Autistic Spectrum
   Disorder (ASD) 36, 40,
   41
  complex profiles 45
 Autistic Continuum
  Disorder vi, 30
  (also see Autistic
   Spectrum Disorder
 Autistic Features 34
Autistic Spectrum
  Disorder (ASD) iv, vi,
  30-44, 45, 50, 52-53,
  64, 65
  adulthood 32
  and vaccines 44
  causes of 31
  and dentist 31
  help and support 42
  identifying 34
  increasing incidence of 30,
   31, 52
 in relation to:
  ADD/ADHD 7, 13, 20,
   21, 25, 26
  Tourette Syndrome 2-5
  Asperger's Syndrome 46,
   48, 49, 50
  intellectual ability 32

learning difficulties
  associated with 32
 medical conditions
  associated with 32
 referring 42
 related conditions/sub-
  groups 34
 understanding the
  condition 30
Autistic tendencies 34

B

Basal ganglia damage/
  dysfunction 50-51, 71
 Causing:
  unusual movements 46
  psychiatric disturbances
   50
Behaviour
 in relation to:
  ADHD 6-21, 22, 23, 24
  Asperger's Syndrome
   46-49
  Autistic Spectrum
   Disorder (ASD) 33,-
   35, 40, 43
  Conduct Disorder 70
  Fetal Alcohol Syndrome
   21
  OCD iv, 2, 3, 4, 45, 50, 71
  Oppositional Defiant
   Disorder 70
  PANDA S 50-51
  Tourette Syndrome 1-5,
   50-51, 71
 Behavioural-management
  techniques 9, 15,

BESD (Behaviour,
  Emotional and Social
  Difficulties) iv
Bipolar Disorder 17
Blaming others, as sign of
  ADHD 22
Body language, interpreting,
  32
Boredom, sign of ADHD 23
Brain
 in relation to:
  ADHD 6, 10-11, 17, 29,
  Basal ganglia damage/
   dysfunction 10, 46, 50-
   51, 71
  Autistic Spectrum
   Disorder 30, 31, 32,
  CFS/ME vii
  Childhood Hemiplegia vi
  OCD 71
  PANDAS 50
Bullying
 in relation to:
  ADHD 8, 9, 23, 24, 70
  Anti-Bullying Campaign
   63
  Asperger's Syndrome 47
  Autistic Spectrum
   Disorder 24, 26
  PANDAS 51
  Tourette Syndrome 4
Bullying
  of children 26
  of children/parents by
   educational and
   medical professionals
   9, 53

C
Caffeine, 53, 64,
  as contributory factor
   in ADHD 8, 66
CAPD (Central Auditory
  Processing Disorder,
  now known as Auditory
  Processing Disorder, see
  Auditory Processing
  Disorder)
Carbohydrates, in relation
  to ADHD 8, 66
Carelessness, as sign of
  ADHD 20
Careers advice 51
Case studies
 in relation to:
  ADHD 17-20,
  Asperger's Syndrome 38,
   50-51, 47-49
  Autistic Spectrum
   Disorder 39, 41-43
  Obsessive Compulsive
   Disorder 3-5, 71
  PANDAS 50-51
  Tourette Syndrome 3-5,
   49, 50-51, 71
 by name:
  Adult with Asperger's
   Syndrome and
   Dyspraxia 33
  DJ 3-4
  John 3, 71,
  Kevin 42
  Kyra 54
  Lisa 41-42
  Louise 50-51
  Paul 47-48

Identification Solutions for Behaviour by Jan Poustie   ISBN 1 901544 82 6

RESOURCES INDEX
(including agencies)